What people are saying about ...

HELP MY UNBELIEF

"Barnabas Piper issues a powerful call to leave the gridlock of black-and-white thinking and enter the gray terrain of second-guessing and doubt. This is where we raise our toughest, most honest questions to God. Such an invitation doesn't push us from the gospel but draws us nearer to the heart of Christ. May we all learn to pray, 'Help my unbelief.'"

Margaret Feinberg, author of *Fight Back with Joy* and *Wonderstruck*

"*Help My Unbelief* gives the church permission to exhale. It's a book that pulls up a chair and looks in the eyes of the doubter and says, 'You're not alone, friend.' Doubt, says Barnabas Piper, is not the antithesis of Faith. Rather, it's a gateway. The key is to ask the right questions, and to be open to God's answers. For this particular disillusioned pastor's daughter, Piper's words are a lifeline—and the key to drawing today's youth back into Christendom."

Emily T. Wierenga, author of five books, including the memoir *Atlas Girl: Finding Home in the Last Place I Thought to Look*; www.emilywierenga.com

"Too often our struggles with doubt are hidden, pushed into the back of the cupboard like a corrosive agent that is too dangerous to touch. With clarity, warmth, and candor, Barnabas Piper shows us that doubt does not have to be something that corrodes, but rather in its right place can be something that strengthens faith."

Mark Sayers, pastor of Red Church in Melbourne, Australia, and author of *Facing Leviathan* and *The Road Trip that Changed the World*

"I'm really excited for you to read Barnabas's new book, *Help My Unbelief: Why Doubt Is Not the Enemy of Faith*. Barnabas writes in a ruthlessly honest and raw way. This book is going to help an entire generation grow and blossom in their faith in the midst of wrestling with doubt."

Derwin L. Gray, lead pastor of Transformation Church and author of *Limitless Life: You Are More Than Your Past When God Holds Your Future*

"In *Help My Unbelief,* Barnabas Piper makes a clear and compelling case for faith amid the sea of doubts many experience in Christianity. It's a necessary book for our generation."

Matt Carter, pastor of preaching at Austin Stone Community Church, Austin, Texas, and coauthor of *The Real Win* and *For the City*

"Barnabas Piper's *Help My Unbelief* is an honest, self-revealing, and engaging treatment of an important subject. This winsome and well-reasoned book avoids clichés and easy, superficial answers. It will benefit many—including those who doubt, those who 'sort of' believe, and those who believe yet long to do so more completely."

Randy Alcorn, author of *Heaven* and *hand in Hand*

"Some Christians have a simple faith unencumbered by doubt. For the rest of us, things aren't so easy. We question. We second-guess. We always want to know why. *Help My Unbelief* is the perfect book for us. With accessible prose and unflinching honesty, Barnabas explores belief that encompasses, is even strengthened by, doubt. Anyone navigating a faith filled with doubts will find Barnabas to be a sympathetic and reliable guide."

Drew Dyck, managing editor of *Leadership Journal* and author of *Yawning at Tigers: You Can't Tame God, So Stop Trying*

"Sometimes believers can give the impression that the Christian life is always one of triumph and confidence. This book by Barnabas Piper counsels us on how to trust God when our faith is weak and wavering. It calls us away from a demon-like faith that simply knows the data about God, to a childlike faith that cries out, 'I believe; help my unbelief.' If you find yourself doubting, or if you love someone who doubts, this book will refresh and encourage."

Russell Moore, president of the Ethics and Religious Liberty Commission and author of *Tempted and Tried: Temptation and the Triumph of Christ*

"Barnabas Piper's *Help My Unbelief* is an encouraging, honest look at an essential but underdiscussed aspect of faith: the tension between belief and unbelief. It's a tension that need not be feared. Piper shows us, rather, how the tension can be healthy and ultimately leave us stronger in our faith. For any believer who has felt alone in their wrestle with unbelief, or who was mistakenly taught that true belief is always ironclad, this valuable and timely book is for you."

Brett McCracken, author of *Gray Matters* and *Hipster Christianity*

Help My Unbelief

WHY DOUBT IS NOT
THE ENEMY OF FAITH

Barnabas Piper

David C Cook®

transforming lives together

HELP MY UNBELIEF
Published by David C Cook
4050 Lee Vance View
Colorado Springs, CO 80918 U.S.A.

David C Cook Distribution Canada
55 Woodslee Avenue, Paris, Ontario, Canada N3L 3E5

David C Cook U.K., Kingsway Communications
Eastbourne, East Sussex BN23 6NT, England

The graphic circle C logo is a registered trademark of David C Cook.

All rights reserved. Except for brief excerpts for review purposes,
no part of this book may be reproduced or used in any form
without written permission from the publisher.

The website addresses recommended throughout this book are offered as a
resource to you. These websites are not intended in any way to be or imply an
endorsement on the part of David C Cook, nor do we vouch for their content.

Unless otherwise marked, all Scripture quotations are taken from The Holy
Bible, English Standard Version® (ESV®), copyright © 2001 by Crossway, a
publishing ministry of Good News Publishers. Used by permission. All rights
reserved. Scripture quotations marked NIV are taken from the Holy Bible, New
International Version®, NIV®. Copyright © 1973, 2011 by Biblica, Inc.® Used by
permission of Zondervan. All rights reserved worldwide. www.zondervan.com.

LCCN 2014959332
ISBN 978-1-4347-0692-8
eISBN 978-1-4347-0934-9

© 2015 Barnabas Piper

The Team: Tim Peterson, Amy Konyndyk, Jack
Campbell, Tiffany Thomas, Karen Athen
Cover Design and Image: Nick Lee

Printed in the United States of America
First Edition 2015

1 2 3 4 5 6 7 8 9 10

043015

For Grace and Dianne:

You will fight unbelief. My hope for you is that when you do, you believe enough to cry, "Help." For when you do, God will answer.

I know this because He has answered me, and He promises to answer those who cry out to Him. He has even answered when I didn't know to cry out.

May you live for Jesus, and may your belief in Him shape everything you do.

Love,
Daddy

CONTENTS

FOREWORD

This book is a tragedy. No, it doesn't end tragically (it is filled with hope), but its very existence is tragic; the author's firsthand experience with the subject matter (doubt and unbelief) is tragic. The need for this book is tragic.

Adam ate the fruit, after all, and the world is now full of broken people with broken emotions and broken minds, looking at the world out of broken eyes. Every human ever born has had a broken relationship with his or her heavenly Father, each urgently in need of mending. Unfortunately, we spend a lot of our time staring at ourselves to see how we feel about Him and acting as if our feelings have any authority over truth and falsehood. As if taking our own temperature tells us anything about God's.

We have a Father who is trustworthy and good, but we stare at His reflection in whatever carnival mirror we might generate, and we fail to connect, to trust ... to truly believe. We struggle to trust Him when things get hard or, as Barnabas Piper describes perfectly in this volume, when things are totally fine and dandy, when we have good families and great churches and whole heaps of head knowledge.

It doesn't matter what all *we* might have; *we* are still broken. We disobey. We fail. We sin. And every sinful act is an act of unbelief, a failure to truly live out what we affirm.

Thank God that our salvation is not dependent on an absence of our own fears. Our failures. Our doubts. In fact, our salvation is not dependent on us at all. It doesn't depend on how we feel. It doesn't depend on how well we answer challenges and questions, and it doesn't depend on how deeply and authentically we really, really feel our answers deep down in our hearts.

Our salvation is on the cross. No matter how broken we may be, no matter how much we might struggle and fail to see and to know the truth (every truth) clearly, we can rest in the One who sees all and knows all. When we cannot see, we are still seen. Even when we stare at our own sputtering joy (and the more we stare, the more it sputters) so intently that we lose sight of the cross, the One on the cross does not lose sight of us.

We are His. We cost Him everything. And His clear eyes will never lose track—or ownership—of what He purchased. His confidence never wanes. Feel how you may, struggle how you may, once bought, once loved with His blood, you cannot slip from His hands.

For those who are His but still doubt, for those who have ever loved Him but disobeyed, the task is as simple as it is impossible for us to do on our own. We are to see as clearly, to love as surely, to rejoice as confidently, and to know the Father as fully as He does.

It is the journey of journeys, the trek we shall never finish, and it begins today, with one foot lifted. Now the other. Repeat. The answer to all your doubts and failures begins here: *You are not the answer. He is.*

Do you want to believe? Then you already do. And that is the beating heart of this book.

Belief is from Him. Ask for it, and in the asking, you have already received.

Do not worry about your own weaknesses. Stop fearing your own sickly reflection and your distressingly philosophical navel. Ignore your empty emotional hands. Those are your qualifications for His grace. His hands are full. And you are in them.

Lord, I believe. Help my unbelief.

And so it will be until the graves are emptied.

N. D. Wilson

INTRODUCTION

"I was born into a Christian home and accepted Jesus at a young age." You've heard this line or something resembling it a thousand times. If you, like me, grew up in a churchgoing family, this was the opening chord to so many testimonies you heard at Sunday school or youth camp or wherever. It was the opening to mine.

I was born to John and Noél Piper on March 31, 1983. My father had been a pastor at Bethlehem Baptist Church in Minneapolis, Minnesota, for almost three years. My birthday fell on Maundy Thursday, a solemn day in the church calendar commemorating the Last Supper. From my very first day I was tied inextricably to the church.

I spent my first thirty years as a pastor's kid, marked by consistent and rigorous scriptural teaching. I knew my Bible inside and out. I was the Sunday school answer man, helped lead youth group worship, and generally looked the part of a good Christian boy. In my book *The Pastor's Kid*,[1] I describe in detail how all this "good Christian" stuff was hollow, though. It wasn't outright hypocrisy or overt rebellion (most of the time). The hollowness came from my lack of belief and inability to even explain what that meant. I thought I believed, but I didn't even know what belief was.

When I was seven years old, I walked into my dad's study at home one day and told him I wanted to follow Jesus. I don't remember why. It might have been fear of hell, it might have been a desire to spend eternity with my family, or it might have been guilt. I sat on his knee and had a conversation also now long forgotten. Then we pulled out my illustrated NIV children's Bible, opened up to a blank page at the beginning, and wrote a profession of faith. My childish hand wrote about my need for a savior and how I believed Jesus was my only hope and now my life would be His forever.

From that day forward I have considered myself a Christian. I know I am a sinner. That much is obvious to anyone who knows me. I believe God is holy, so much so that He cannot abide sin in His presence. I believe I cannot do a single thing to purify myself enough to gain access to God. I believe that "God so loved the world, that he gave his only Son, that whoever believes in him should not perish but have eternal life."[2] And I believe in the perfect Son, Jesus, the only man who ever lived a life of perfection and thus was able to be the flawless sacrifice and bear God's punishment for my sin and those of everyone else who believes. I believe Jesus rose from the dead and thus has shown Himself to be the conquering King who will one day return to "wipe away every tear" and reside in a newly created earth where "neither shall there be mourning, nor crying, nor pain anymore."[3]

I have believed these truths almost all my life. And yet …

And yet I have committed sins that have deeply wounded others and nearly destroyed my relationship with Jesus.

And yet I have looked Scripture full in the face and decided my way is better than God's; I would rather be my own god.

And yet I doubt the promises God gave even though He provided the surety: His beloved Son's very life. My troubles are bigger than God's love no matter what He says.

And yet I am skeptical. I know what Scripture says and I know the arguments, but the questions stack up. Some people think, *God says it, I believe it, that settles it.* But it doesn't settle it. Did God really say it? I don't really believe it. Nothing is settled.

And yet my belief is weak. Or maybe it's not there. Or maybe I don't really know what belief means. And that's what this book is about. *What is belief?*

You have your own "and yet." Maybe yours inserted itself before you even professed belief; all the claims of the Bible and this man, Jesus, are just too much to assent to. You struggle with questions of evil and pain and the existence of God. You are a skeptic, either willfully or because you just can't help it. I cannot answer all your questions. I don't think anyone on earth can. But answers exist. They are found in belief, with or without empirical evidence to back them up. I hope to show you that it's worth it to risk believing.

Or maybe your "and yet" is on the other end of the spectrum; you have so willingly followed Jesus that you have never raised a question about life's hardships or God's promises. You follow blindly but faithfully. But is this because you truly believe without doubt or because you fear where questions might take you? Are you afraid that questioning or even, gulp, *doubting* might open a Pandora's box of sin and judgment? My goal is to help you see that belief isn't blind faith and that questions, if asked well, are building blocks for stronger faith rather than stepping-stones away from it.

If your "and yet" lies somewhere in the middle or is some combination of both, this book will still help you by exploring belief from both ends. It will look at "I believe" and "help my unbelief," the expression of a desperate man in Mark 9. These juxtaposed phrases represent the reality of every follower of Jesus no matter how mature, new, stumbling, or strong. We believe. And we don't. We follow. We fail. We are weak, and we need help.

In these pages I hope you find words to bolster your belief. No amount of belief moves us beyond "help my unbelief." Rather the stronger our belief, the more urgent our plea. I pray you will be encouraged and challenged, cut down and built up. I pray you will see the frailty of your belief and the strength of what you believe in. And I pray that belief will be more than an assertion; may it be a living thing in your soul that shapes and drives you in all you do.

Chapter 1

TENSION

No one could help the boy. The demon was destroying him with seizures and fits that flung him into fire and water. His father was desperate. He loved his son and would move heaven and earth to save him; if he could not find a way to help his boy, he would lose him. The man heard of a teacher, a teacher who walked on water, calmed storms with a word, and even raised the dead. But the teacher did something more. He looked demons in the eye and banished them with a word; the man knew because the teacher had done it to a whole swarm of demons by sending them into a herd of pigs that immediately turned tail and rushed into the sea to drown. If anyone could help his son, this teacher could.

The father took his scarred and frail son and found Jesus, or rather found His followers. He asked them for help, but they could do nothing. In his fear and hurt, the man became angry and spoke harshly to the followers. Defensive and ashamed of their powerlessness, they lashed back. Just then Jesus arrived. Mark's epistle tells the story of what happened next:

> And they brought the boy to him. And when the spirit saw him, immediately it convulsed the boy, and he fell on the ground and rolled about, foaming at the mouth. And Jesus asked his father,

"How long has this been happening to him?" And he said, "From childhood. And it has often cast him into fire and into water, to destroy him. But if you can do anything, have compassion on us and help us." And Jesus said to him, "'If you can'! All things are possible for one who believes." Immediately the father of the child cried out and said, "I believe; help my unbelief!" And when Jesus saw that a crowd came running together, he rebuked the unclean spirit, saying to it, "You mute and deaf spirit, I command you, come out of him and never enter him again." And after crying out and convulsing him terribly, it came out, and the boy was like a corpse, so that most of them said, "He is dead." But Jesus took him by the hand and lifted him up, and he arose.[1]

More than any other story in Scripture, this one exhibits the Christian experience of belief. It doesn't explain it or clarify it. It doesn't describe it or give direction. Instead, it captures the experience perfectly. At first blush, this story has little to do with our daily lives. We live in a decidedly natural state with tangible lives. Most of us live modern, technologically driven lives in the Western world, and this story seems almost fanciful and a bit frightening. It's the kind of thing that happened long ago in a galaxy far, far away. After all, it's the story of an exorcism but without the Hollywood flair and excitement of Linda Blair spewing out pea soup and oatmeal.[2] In this real-life exorcism, the Son of God exercised His power and exorcised a demon. Victory was had, and a boy was saved. But as with so much of Scripture there is something more here. In fact, a single sentence from this story holds the keys to the mystery of belief.

On my right forearm I have a tattoo. I'd long heard the advice "Don't get a tattoo unless it's something you want on you forever." I took this advice to heart as a teen and through most of my twenties. It saved me from a handful of potentially embarrassing decisions. (Remember when barbed wire tats were popular? I don't have one.) I got my tattoo a couple of weeks before my thirtieth birthday. I was old enough to know better and to know exactly what I was doing. I had lived enough life to find something I wanted permanently inked on my body. It isn't art. It isn't flashy—just simple script serving as a reminder my soul needs to see every day.

"I believe; help my unbelief."

In my midtwenties I went through what rightly could be called a crisis of faith—a true test of whether I should devote my life to what I grew up believing about Jesus. I was faced with the decision of walking away from it all, because that would be the easier thing to do, or turning to Jesus and giving Him all of my life. (I'll share more about this later.) For most of my life I had felt the pull, the tension of faith. I had felt the draw of sin and given in often. I believed in Jesus, but I doubted. I believed in Jesus, but I didn't. Then one day I stumbled across this story from Mark. I'd read it dozens of times, but this time it grabbed me. That one sentence grabbed me.

The father's words gripped my heart with a vicelike power. In five words he explained so much of the Christian's experience, of my experience. That simple sentence is the key to the struggles, the ups and downs, the winding road of belief. In a breath he expressed the highest of heights, the strength of virtue, the emptiness of doubt, and the yearning for something on to which he could hold. He spoke of being pulled in two opposite directions, one of peace and the other of chaos and fear. And he spoke of clinging, holding fast, knowing to whom he should look. All this in five little words.

SEESAWS AND TUG-OF-WAR

Christians who don't know the tension of "I believe; help my unbelief" might not be Christians at all, or at the least they might be very infantile ones. Our faith is one of brutal tensions. Not everyone can express this, but every Christian knows it. We feel it in our guts. We feel the motion of the up and down and down and up. We feel as if we're going to bust in half as we're pulled in two directions at once. To not recognize the significance of these words indicates a simplistic, thoughtless belief. It isn't a mark of maturity but rather of not being mature enough to know our own weakness and need. Tension is our state of being for all of this life, and to live as a believer is to live in it.

We are born sinners incapable of making ourselves pleasing to God yet called to be holy as God is holy.

We are finite creatures seeking to understand an infinite God.

We trust that God is good although the world He created and sovereignly rules is filled with badness.

We think in terms of scientific evidence, proof, and logic though our holy book tells of miracles and supernatural occurrences.

We believe God is omnipresent though we can see Him nowhere.

We have one God in three persons but not three gods.

We defy the economy of earthly power by following a leader who died to save us, who willingly laid down His glory and power, and who calls us to be the least in order to be great.

We live in this world but are told it is not our home; we are not of this place.

Our king came and ushered in His kingdom but then left with a promise of His return. So we wait.

We are saved by faith, not by good or moral works. But faith without good and moral works is dead.

We are called to consider suffering as joy.

We follow the teachings of a book that is in part clear and in part mysterious and enigmatic.

Each of these tensions holds true for every Christian. They ebb, flow, spike, and ease off, but they're always present. At points they have overwhelmed me, and other times they have hardened me because they seemed too much to accept. And all the time I feel the roiling of the seesaw's rise and fall. My heart plays tug-of-war with me, sometimes over doubts and other times over sin. I trust but not as I should, not always. I obey but not as I ought, not always.

I don't take many things at face value; I question nearly everything. The upside of this is that I'm curious and love to learn. The downside is that I am a cynic who trusts my own impressions and opinions instead of trusting others'. This meant that as a child and into my teens, I found it easy to disregard teachers or even my parents. I wasn't usually rebellious, just dismissive (though often with a snide retort thrown in to show my wit and wisdom). As I grew older, this questioning turned into a subtle sort of pride; I saw myself as the arbiter of truth in my own life. I *knew* the Bible was true. I knew all the answers about theology, faith, and the Christian life. But underneath it all was that pride giving me the permission to ignore what I knew, to give in to greed and lust and dishonesty.

And as sin does, it fed my doubts about others and fed my confidence in myself. At no point, though, did God ever let me forget Him or leave Him completely. At one level I *did* believe, I did know, I did follow. I wasn't throwing myself into sin; I was simply accepting sin in my otherwise Christian life. I wanted to be a follower of Jesus, and I wanted to be a follower of Barnabas. I believed and I doubted. Back and forth, back and forth. And in the end, here I stand. I believe; help my unbelief.

AS IT SHOULD BE

> We are so impressed by the scientific clank ... that we feel we ought not to say that the sunflower turns because it knows where the sun is. It is almost second nature to us to prefer explanations ... with a large vocabulary. We are much more comfortable when we are assured that the sunflower turns because it is heliotropic.
>
> The trouble with that kind of talk is that it ... tempts us to think that we really know what the sunflower is up to. But we don't. The sunflower is a mystery, just as every single thing in the universe is.[3]
>
> —Robert Farrar Capon

In the post-Enlightenment Western world, we live by rules of science. Theories are posed, evidence is gathered, facts are disputed, and in the end, truth is discovered. At least truth about some things is discovered. But the model of scientific discovery simply does not apply to much of life. One of the not-so-subtle tenets of Enlightenment thinking is the disregard for the supernatural and the subsequent magnification of mankind. Man has superseded deity as the primary force and value in the world. We can see this even in the gut reaction to the story I shared from Mark earlier. When we hear of demons and exorcisms, they don't seem present or real. They seem more like tales of dragons and ghouls and knights in shining armor. To put stock in such fanciful stories, according to many, has the same value (at best) as finding the morals in the Grimms' fairy tales.

To many modern thinkers, though, belief in God and a holding to religion are akin to intentional stupidity. Faith is built, they say, on tradition and custom taking hold of our minds and a refusal to think in any other direction. (In some cases they are correct, but that is hardly a fair characterization.) Because they cannot see God or plausible evidence of His being, to believe in Him is outright madness. To them, believing in God is like holding fast to the Easter Bunny or Santa Claus.

> I had therefore to remove knowledge in order to make room for belief.[4]
>
> —Immanuel Kant

> I have found it an amusing strategy, when asked whether I am an atheist, to point out that the

questioner is also an atheist when considering Zeus, Apollo, Amon Ra, Mithras, Baal, Thor, Wotan, the Golden Calf and the Flying Spaghetti Monster. I just go one god further.[5]

—Richard Dawkins

God does not fit the world as Western thinkers have shaped it. He does not fit the processes and grids of theory, evidence, and proof. So, under the influence of Enlightenment philosophers, society relegates Him to those second-tier statuses of religious tradition, personal values, and vague spirituality.

The God of the Bible, though, will not be relegated to anything. He is the omnipotent creator of all, including all those who are doing the relegating. It's important that we see Him as the God "of the Bible," too, because that is how He has chosen to explain and reveal Himself to us. If you are a Christian, what you know of God comes from the Bible; it is the breathed-out revelation from the heart of God to the hands of man. If you are not a Christian and think of the Bible as something less, a work of great literature or a book of mythology for example, you will likely take umbrage with much of what I write. I believe the Bible to be completely true because I believe it to be the actual *word* of God throughout. Is it circular to believe in a book because it came from God and believe in God because of what that book says about Him? I suppose, in a sense. But there is more to the story than that. Bear with me. All viewpoints and beliefs have presuppositions. Yours do. Mine do. Here are mine.

What the Bible reveals of God is precisely what God wanted revealed of Himself, no more and no less. But it isn't everything about

Him. Scripture raises as many questions as it answers. It asks the impossible and describes the miraculous. The Bible tells stories that are grotesque and stories that are heartwarming. Parts of it are horrifying and others are befuddling. It is written in multiple genres and has thousands of characters. In short, it is representative of the real world and God's relationship with it, not a book to simplify the world so we can understand it all. And it is just the way God wanted it.

This should tell us something both about God and about belief. God is infinite, beyond our understanding, and He chose to reveal Himself to us in a way that sparks questions rather than settles all of them. God did not want us to have easy instructions and simple answers. He didn't want us to be able to understand Him so well that we could package Him, wrap Him up, and put a bow on Him. (Of course, many in the evangelical church try their hardest to accomplish just this. They want a God who can be understood in full and explained systematically. They fail to recognize the meaning of the terms *infinite* and *omnipotent*. God cannot be grasped, not in full, and that's what makes Him God.) If we could store God in a box, what about Him would be worthy of worship? In fact, God *could not* do such a thing; He could not shrink Himself, His profound and unfathomable self, to a size our human minds and hearts could grasp. He wanted us to search, to wrestle, to wonder, to be mystified. He wanted us to *ask*.

ASKING

Much of belief is asking: asking for help as the father in Mark 9 did, asking for understanding, asking why, asking when. I have two young daughters, and they show their belief in me by asking things of me. "Can I have a snack?" indicates they believe I can provide them with Goldfish crackers or Oreos. "Why are the stars big balls of fire but only look like dots to us?" shows their belief that I can explain scientific facts. "Why do you and Mommy have to kiss around us?" shows, well, that mostly shows disgust. Questions are an indication of trust. Or they can be.

The Bible tells us to have faith like a child. Children are perpetual questioners, but they're also perpetual believers. They ask, then eagerly await an answer. They mull over the answer, then fire another question if it doesn't make sense to them. Questions are the conversational currency of a child. Every question is asked to learn, out of a desire to understand, from a stance of trust. Children ask not to challenge but in order to believe. That's a big part of what "faith like a child" means.

Questions indicate belief only if you actually want an answer. Someone who asks without wanting to learn is not truly asking, but is challenging. Challenging is not believing, but undermining. A researcher asks questions to learn the facts, find the patterns, and create a hypothesis or theory. She wants to find the truth. In a cross-examination a prosecutor asks questions in order to reveal a lie. He is challenging, not really asking. The main difference is whether the questioner has an answer in mind already or desires to hear what answer will be offered. Researchers might have theories, but their questions are to test those theories by finding out the real answers. Prosecutors have answers they want to hear. An unexpected answer is not acceptable. They know what they want and need to hear, and their questions are designed to lead to those responses.

God is infinite. While the finite human mind can understand aspects of His character, even those cannot be understood in full. His bigness is too big, His goodness too good, His wrath too terrible, His grace too profound, His knowledge too deep. Because of this, God is inherently mysterious to us. We simply cannot fathom the fullness, or even a portion of the fullness, of who He is or what He does. We cannot fit Him into our proofs and evidentiary structures. By revealing what He did in Scripture, God created a massive mystery. He gave us an enigma, a puzzle, a riddle with so many dimensions and plotlines and layers and themes that even just those sixty-six books have generated libraries of volumes of thought, argument, and questions.

Belief is not a black-and-white endeavor built on simple truths. It is the exploration of a great mystery girded by great truths. I have often heard it said that "the Bible says it, I believe it, that settles it," as if that is all there is to belief and being a Christian. For those of us who grew up in a traditional Sunday school context or a more fundamentalist, legalistic background, we recognize that general attitude about faith and God. "What does the Bible say? Well, just do that thing!" But the Bible isn't clear all the time. It isn't a simplistic, comprehensive rule book (thank God!), and it doesn't address every problem explicitly. Instead, it depicts the character and work of God. The Bible tells a narrative of creation, fall, promise, redemption, and glory. In that narrative are lessons and declarations of great truth, but there are also allusions and suggestions of truth. God's character is described, discernible at points, but also inscrutable. Because of His infinity, His character baffles us even while it comforts and directs us. That is the mystery and the truth, hand in hand. The Bible gives everything we need but not every answer; all the necessary truth but plenty of room to wonder.

So in order to truly believe, we must ask and ask and ask. We must ask as a researcher asks. Sure, we can have our theories, but we must also be willing to adjust or abandon them if the answers revealed to us prove those theories wrong. We must ask as a little child asks, full of curiosity. When an answer doesn't make sense, keep asking. And believe that there is an answer.

But we cannot become the prosecutor. We cannot put "God in the dock" to be cross-examined, as C. S. Lewis described it. In his famous collection of essays by that name, Lewis explained and defended God's character and work as if society had put God on trial. If we are certain of our beliefs and cross-examine God to prove our views, we have failed. That is not belief. Not only are we likely wrong, but also we have reversed the roles. God is the One with the true story; we are not. He is the One who knows all; we are not. (Check out Job 38–41 for the best biblical example of God putting a cross-examiner in his place.)

And we cannot ask as an older child asks either. Older children begin to think they know better than their parents. My daughters aren't quite there yet, but they'll reach that point soon enough. An older child asks questions to stump her parents or to challenge authority. She no longer implicitly believes her parents to be wise and all-knowing, trustworthy in every circumstance. Of course, parents aren't all-wise, so the child's skepticism is often proved out to a point. Not so with God. We never get to a place where we know more or are in a position to question His authority. Our skepticism toward God will never bear out anything other than disappointment and hurt for ourselves.

ASKING WELL

To ask well[6] we must ask with a willingness to receive an answer. We can't have an agenda or ulterior motive. We can't ask as the prosecutor or adolescent asks. Good asking is honest asking. Belief is built on this kind of asking because this kind of asking is built on trust. But that doesn't mean it is passive asking.

To ask well is to examine as far as we can. If the answer we find doesn't seem right the first few times—or few hundred times—we continue to ask. We find better questions, more pointed and specific. We look at different angles of the issue and try to see all sides. We become a combination of a young child curious about everything and a detective sleuthing for the truth.

But asking well also means knowing when to lay our questions down. Sometimes there simply aren't answers, at least not at the time. It's unlikely we ever forget our questions, but we must know when to shelve them. Maybe a time comes when we take them back out, or maybe this lifetime provides no answers. If we don't put away some questions, they will end up eating our beliefs from the inside out. We will begin to fixate on the vacuum where answers "should" be and think of God as unsatisfactory because He has failed to provide for that "should."

We can question well and be in inexpressible pain. Think of Elisabeth Elliot whose husband, Jim, was martyred in South America in 1956 as he and four friends tried to reach the Huaorani people of Ecuador. Her response was very human: pain, anguish, questions. But she had this to say: "Waiting on God requires the willingness to bear uncertainty, to carry within oneself the unanswered question, lifting the heart to God about it whenever it intrudes upon one's thoughts."[7] Elliot did not cease asking even when answers weren't readily apparent. She took her questions full of hurt to God. She asked even as she believed.

We can question well and feel utterly lost. We can question well and not know whether God has answers for us. No greater example than Jesus shows us this. More than any person in history, He faced questions that could not or would not be answered the way He wanted, yet He pressed on in the belief, the knowledge, that God was doing good. In the garden of Gethsemane Jesus wept and pleaded, "Father, if you are willing, take this cup from me; yet not my will, but yours be done."[8] As He gave up His life for us, as He suffered on the cross, He cried out, "My God, my God, why have you forsaken me?"[9] Jesus, more than anyone in history, knew God's character and power and goodness. Yet still He asked. And Jesus, more than you, more than me, more than everyone, felt the weight of suffering and pain and doubt because He actually felt the weight of everyone's suffering and pain and doubt. Yet still He believed. He is the perfect example of questioning in faith.

But when our questions begin to undermine commitment to God, that is unbelief, and that is when it is time to examine whether we are, in fact, asking well. We cannot question well and turn our backs on God. We cannot question as the rich young man from Matthew 19 did when he asked Jesus, "What must I do to have eternal life?" then walked away disappointed because the answer did not suit him.[10] And aren't we all like that? Don't we all question God, then turn our backs on Him when we don't like His response? Atheists often say they reject God because they cannot reconcile Him with the reality around them, but somewhere in them is the inability to reconcile themselves to believing and obeying. Questioning isn't just about the intellectual understanding of who God is; it is about the willingness to follow what God commands. Often the intellectual obstacle to belief is a convenient excuse for rebellion. So when we ask, we must desire to both hear the answer and *accept* the answer. If we don't understand it, at the very least we understand from whom it came. And He can certainly be believed.

PRESUPPOSING BELIEF

I mentioned earlier that no argument can be made objectively; we always have presuppositions. I write with a number of presuppositions in these pages. I presuppose God's existence and sovereign goodness. I presuppose the authority of the Bible and that it's God's word. I presuppose truth and that God's word is the foundation for it. But I presuppose something even more basic than those: belief itself.

I presuppose that it is real and attainable. I presuppose that it is valuable and worthy of pursuit. I presuppose that certain things and people are worth believing in.

Of course, I will do my best to support these presuppositions and explain them. Not all presuppositions are created equal; some of mine came to me in adulthood, while others I was born into before discarding and then later rediscovering them. Presuppositions *are* beliefs that are held foundationally under other beliefs. Sometimes they are subtle and we don't even recognize their presence. They are the beliefs that allow for or exclude other beliefs. They can be helpful or harmful. In this book about belief I feel it's important to acknowledge up front their presence and effect and to state where I am coming from. I do not assume all who read this book presuppose the same things I do, and I respect that, so I will try to address other starting points and stances along the way.

Chapter 2

WHAT IS BELIEF?

By the time I left home for college I knew everything a Christian kid should know. I had memorized numerous passages of Scripture and could recite the Ten Commandments, the Beatitudes, the Romans Road, and so on. I knew all the Bible stories and all the biblical morals. I knew sex outside of marriage was wrong and porn was wrong. I knew I should go to church and read my Bible and pray. I knew the doctrine of the Trinity and all five *solas*—*sola fide, sola gratia, solus Christus, sola Scriptura*, and *soli Deo gloria*—those pillar doctrines of the Reformation that defined true Christianity (and I even knew basically what they meant too).[1] I knew that good works wouldn't get me to heaven; only faith in Jesus would do that. I knew that Jesus was the Son of God, that I was a sinner, and that I needed His perfect life and death and resurrection to atone for my sins. (And yes, I knew what *atonement* meant too.) But I also knew that good works were evidence of that faith and they mattered a lot. I even knew theological nuance and what terms such as *soteriology, pneumatology*, and *ecclesiology* meant.

I would have said I believed in Jesus Christ as my Savior and followed Him as Lord. And at some level I did. But something was missing. My "belief" lacked the power of conviction, the force and reality to make me move. I cognitively believed, and that directed and shaped much of my life. However, there were portions of my life that, though I called Jesus "Lord," I did not let Him rule. Those areas were where I kept my hidden sins: lust (often just a Christian-ish euphemism for pornography), lying, theft. And it had been that way since I was a child.

I didn't fall into these sins. It wasn't the kind of thing where I got caught up in something really bad. I wasn't leading a double life. At least not at first. I was just a normal kid, the kind who's inclined to do his own thing and test authority. In fact, I often confessed sin to God and to friends (after all, that was the youth group thing to do). After I confessed to a sin, I would change, but the change wasn't really change because I was believing in me to make the difference instead of believing God to make the difference in me. That is a vain endeavor, and over time it becomes less of an endeavor altogether. That's what happens when we work without belief in something, some*one*, greater than ourselves. We give up.

Was my belief real? Did I, in fact, believe? To rightly answer that question we have to define what belief is. My aim in "defining" belief is not to offer the be-all and end-all realities of it, but to frame it in such a way that we understand it well. I want to give legs to the term *belief* so that when we use it we mean something useful.

BELIEF LIKE A DEMON'S

One of the scariest realities in the world—or at least one that should be scary—for a professing Christian is found in the Bible.

> You believe that God is one; you do well. Even the demons believe—and shudder!
>
> —James 2:19

In our modern, "enlightened" world we don't speak much of demons or pay them much mind (or even believe they exist). But in much of the developing world their presence is both felt and seen. These workers of Satan did not cease to exist after the Bible was completed.[2] Evil as they are, demons "believe" good doctrine. They believe the reality of God. And it makes them shudder. A demon is irredeemable, condemned, an enemy of God. It is utterly evil, through and through, yet it believes right things about God. If a demon can "believe" in God, what does that mean for my belief?

This question ought to bring our comfortable, apathetic Christian lives to a screeching halt. We call ourselves believers. Even in telling my story I have written of "believing" in all sorts of doctrinal tenets. But what does that even mean? Do we believe in the same way demons do? If yes, Lord, help us and show us how to change. If not, how so?

My wife and I had a difficult start to marriage. Among intense family conflicts, our own immaturity, and some poor choices, we didn't exactly head into marital bliss. We loved each other, but that wasn't enough to smooth out the challenges. We had our first child very early, and as near kids ourselves, we were stretched to the limit. We had yet to figure out how to be married before we were learning how to be parents. God gave us a beautiful baby girl, and we poured ourselves into her, but that left less time and energy than we would have wanted to devote to each other. It was a trying time. The kind of trying time God uses to grow and mature people.

But a person has to want to grow for such times to really bear fruit. In spite of what should have been a humbling experience, I was arrogant. I rested in my knowledge about God and the Bible combined with a theology degree from a respected Christian college. Instead of letting God teach me and shape me through my circumstances and my mistakes, I took the lessons I felt I needed and moved on. I put myself in a position to decide what I needed instead of actually recognizing my own deep needs.

During this time we began meeting with a couple from church, Mark and Dianne, who counseled and mentored us. Without them, I don't know if our marriage would have survived those painful months. Mark is an incredibly patient and wise man who cared deeply for me and gave much of himself throughout this period of time to help me grow (as did Dianne for my wife; she was so significant, in fact, that we named our second daughter after her). He would share biblical and practical wisdom with me, and my most common response was "I know." Always "I know." We would discuss the gospel and how it should shape our lives, and I would respond with something like "I believe all that." After the hundredth or thousandth such response, Mark stopped, looked at me, and said, "Barnabas, you keep saying 'I know' and 'I believe that,' but really you just mentally assent to what I'm telling you. That kind of belief is not the same as *really* believing."

And shouldn't I have known this? I said I believed one thing and acted in opposition to the belief. I could have humbled myself, seen my great need, and begun learning what it meant to follow Jesus. I should have seen the disparity between what my mouth said and what my life indicated. Instead, I decided I knew best what I needed to learn, took it, and went on my way. I believed. But I didn't *believe*.

Mental assent is not belief. It is part of belief, but not the whole of it. What I knew to be true about the Bible, God's grace, obedience, and repentance was mental assent, but it did not transform me. It influenced me, sure. It kept me in the realm of right and the neighborhood of Christlike. But I was not transformed. Almost every church kid assents to the teachings of Scripture both doctrinally and morally. But, as I did, many harbor hidden sins rather than being shaped by their belief, letting it fill all the voids and vacancies of life. It is belief that recognizes and even expresses truth but cares nothing for it. We believe like demons believe.

FAITH AND BELIEF

> He does not believe who does not live according to his belief.[3]
>
> —Thomas Fuller

What makes the difference between the belief of a demon and the belief of a follower of Jesus? What gives belief the power to make us *do* instead of just think and acknowledge? How do we live according to our beliefs? One might think it's willpower, but that well runs dry quickly. One might think it's greater understanding, a deeper look into the nature and tenets of the beliefs. But do we really think that our study will show us more than what a demon already knows? Unlikely. No, what gives us the ability to live what we believe is one word: *transformation.*

Transformed is the word I used just a few sentences ago to describe what I needed to move me from in the neighborhood of Christlike to actually following Christ with all my life. Transformation was what was missing from my belief; it is what is missing from so much of the church's belief as well. Belief that collects knowledge and acknowledges something to be true but doesn't transform one's actions is the mere mental-assent part. Christianity is built on transformational belief. In Acts 16:31, Paul told the Philippian jailer, "Believe in the Lord Jesus, and you will be saved." Belief leading to salvation must be more than mere knowledge. Something must change; a fundamental shift must happen.

That sort of belief is what the Bible calls faith. Faith is what differentiates a Christian from a demon. Faith is belief that trans-forms into action, into new actions. Faith is what a child has in her parents, and we know this because she lives it. She doesn't fret about her daily needs because her parents provide for them. She contentedly plays because she knows Mom or Dad will take care of the big stuff. She runs and flings herself at Dad when he comes home from a business trip because she knows he'll catch her. Those simple, content actions are belief in action, faith.

In the same way that for a child the object of faith is her parents, for a Christian it is God. The object of someone's faith is formative. A skydiver has faith in her parachute, so she jumps. She had faith in the airplane and the pilot, so she boarded. The objects of her faith shaped her actions. So it is with God, but connected to all of life, not just individual actions. He is what we believe *in*, and that is of infinite significance. It means He determines the course our faith takes, what it looks like, how it plays out. It means He is the standard for our actions and our thoughts. Children look to parents for motivation, input, direction, and a standard. We look to God.

When all we have is the mental-assent part of belief, though, we base our actions on some other standard: our emotions, our happiness, our stresses. We know there is a higher standard, but only cognitively, not transformationally. What we know about God is not the same thing as believing in Him and having that transforming faith. In fact, it can even be a deterrent because mental assent so easily substitutes for real life change.

This was the trap I fell into. My knowledge fooled me and those around me. In church I could answer all the questions from teachers. When I met with youth pastors or mentors and they would dig into my life with probing questions, I knew just what to say, the right answers. It wasn't an act. It was knowledge. I knew and believed what I said. I just didn't live it all. When I did something wrong, I would admit it, apologize for it, and talk of repentance and a need for grace. But instead of true repentance, the kind that actually depends on God's grace to transform, I would simply do right for a while and fall back into sin. I wasn't trying to be hypocritical; I was blinded by the truth I knew. I had fooled myself into thinking I was living by faith in God, when instead I was living a life shaped by knowledge of Him. And those are very different things.

Even today one of my greatest struggles is refusing to let my knowledge of God stand in the place of genuine faith in God. Sometimes I can barely tell a difference. Am I speaking from conviction or from a head full of knowledge? Am I acting rightly out of a sense of moral obligation and knowing it's "the right thing to do" or out of a life that seeks to honor Christ? Am I speaking the truth out of love or out of a desire to impress? Motives are rarely clean and pure. It is difficult to delineate, especially since knowledge is *part* of faith. But the difference shows up in how I feel about my actions. If I find joy in honoring Christ when nobody notices, it is real. If I stand by what I said because I believe it to be true and right instead of waffling, offering caveats, or backing down, it is real. If I find joy in one person being blessed by what I say or write instead of needing acclaim, it is real. In the end, faith looks like Jesus and knowledge looks like something a whole lot hollower and uglier.

For me, and others like me who grew up steeped in Christian teaching, learning to recognize the difference doesn't usually happen through a lesson or a sermon. After all, we are full up on those. Change happens through seeing Jesus, through having our hearts opened along with our minds. Maybe this happens through crisis. Maybe it happens through failure. Maybe it happens through conversation with friends. Sometimes it happens like flipping on a light switch, and other times it happens like the sun rising, where the light creeps in until all of a sudden you realize you can see. No matter how it takes place, though, it always happens through God transforming our hearts to live for Him and through Him.

And this happens to varying degrees for everyone. For me, there were hidden places of my life where I kept sin tucked away, untouched by belief. I partitioned my life and rationalized those hidden places in order to keep transformation at bay because often transformation hurts. Some people lead entire double lives. And every believer struggles to give some area of life to God. Our faith is real but not whole, genuine but not pervasive. I envy Christians who have a simple and profound faith. They may know little of theology proper or technical arguments, but they have a deep knowledge of God Himself and it shapes their lives in full. Their belief is fully transformational. It is true faith.

THE REALEST BELIEF

As we've seen, *belief* means a range of things and can be used in a variety of ways. I believe my wife when she tells me something. I don't believe the Minnesota Vikings will win a Super Bowl in my lifetime. I believe in a thing called love. I don't believe in Santa Claus. Each of these statements is easy to understand by its context. But when people say they believe in God, what does that mean?

It may mean they believe God exists in some form. It may mean they acknowledge God's moral standard as a general guideline. Or it may mean they believe fully in God's word and God's way and look to Him as the object of their faith. While each of these is an accurate statement and a proper use of the term *belief*, only one of them is real belief. That is the third use.

It is real because it is the sort of belief that makes up faith, and faith is what shapes a life. We can believe in God in the other two senses with no faith whatsoever, but the third use of belief is the makings of real faith. Faith cannot exist without it; it would be empty of any substance, faith in nothing. But when we believe completely in the reality of God and the rightness of His word and way, it will give a shape and direction to our lives. The effects will be visible.

Faith isn't the ability to believe long and far into the misty future. It's simply taking God at His word and taking the next step.[4]

—Joni Eareckson Tada

This is the kind of belief Christians seek. It is not a black-and-white belief, either present or not. It is more like the sun. Some days it will shine brightly and shed God's light on and through all of your life. Other times it will be obscured by clouds of distraction, by our delusions of belief (mental assent), by fear or doubt, or by something else. But being obscured doesn't mean it is doused. Sometimes it just takes time to break through those clouds. And like the sun, belief burns hotter in certain seasons of life than others. As Christians, we yearn for an endless summer of bright, warm belief.

For many Christians, though, we go through all the seasons. We go through the frigid, cloudy depths of winter when belief shines through only enough to remind us that it's still real and that warmer, sunnier times will come. We go through times when we don't see the sun for days or weeks because the cloud cover is thick. But real belief always shines through eventually, sometimes in blazing glory and sometimes in subtler hues.

It shines through because its object is imminent and immovable. Belief is only as real as what is believed in and what impact it has on our lives. When belief is brilliantly shining, that is God shining through the believer. Belief leads to faith, and faith is the means by which God shows up, whether it is big or small. That is why the realest belief is that which is wholly and unreservedly in God.

DIFFERENT KINDS OF KNOWING

Belief must be based on something. It might be something cognitive or something instinctive. It might be experiential or it might be intellectual. But we do not believe in things baselessly (though sometimes we believe in them based on something false). When I wrote earlier that knowing about God could be a deterrent to real belief, I meant it. But that is not to say that knowing about God is a bad thing, because not knowing about Him is an even greater deterrent to belief. In fact, not knowing about God makes belief an impossibility.

Just as there are different kinds of belief, there are also different kinds of knowledge. My problem was that I collected knowledge about God the way one collects books. I had a library of information I could use to handle different situations. What I was missing was the knowledge of God like I have of my wife, the relational knowledge that allows me to know instinctively her moods, what will make her laugh, when she needs chocolate (days that end in *y*), when to shut my mouth (admittedly I get that one wrong often), and when to speak up. I can order for her at restaurants and pick which movies to see. It is a relational knowledge between two people who love one another.

Book knowledge of God, if left at that, leads to hollow belief in God. Relational knowledge of God leads to transformational, living belief. So by all means, study God's Word. But don't do so to collect knowledge. Do so to know *Him*. Devoted husbands don't just happen to pick up on things their wives enjoy; they seek them out. In a sense they study their wives, not as subject matter, but to learn how to respect them, please them, surprise them, help them, and make them happy. This is a different sort of knowledge, a deeper knowledge than the kind that can recite facts and offer descriptions. It comes through knowing a person inside and out, knowing that person's character and personality. Such knowledge is the kind that shapes and transforms a life whether in relation to a spouse or God. It is what we should seek in Scripture, because through such knowledge our belief will grow stronger and realer.

Chapter 3

WHAT CAN WE
KNOW ABOUT GOD?

People love mysteries. Millions of Americans sit enraptured by *CSI,* *24, Lost, Sherlock,* and numerous other mysteries. We eat up books by David Baldacci, John Grisham, and more classic authors such as Agatha Christie. We binge watch TV shows on Netflix because we can't abide having to wait to see what happens next. Mysteries intrigue and absorb us.

Here's a question: Would we love mysteries if we couldn't solve them? Imagine the bad guys getting away, the court cases being thrown out, the crimes going unsolved. Those would make awful endings to stories. We want closed cases and no commercial breaks.

We bring these same expectations to belief, to our interactions with God. We bring our questions and expect answers. Every query toward or about God ought to be resolved in an orderly fashion with every thread tied off neatly. We turn the pages of our Bibles expecting to find answers to our questions, and often they are there. But what happens when we can't find them? What happens when we come across an unsolvable mystery about God, a theological conundrum, or something about Him we just don't like? Why did He devote entire cities to destruction in the Old Testament, including all the women and children? If He chooses who will be saved, then why are all unchosen people held responsible for their actions and His choice? Why are my daughters perfectly healthy but my neighbor's child suffered severe birth defects? I prayed, but nothing seemed to happen. If God thinks so highly of marriage, why do so many Christian couples get divorced? Why doesn't He help them? And this list could go on and on.

If you are like me, your first reaction will be to answer these questions, to put your knowledge into play and try to button them up tight. But it won't work. Your answers may convey some truth, but they won't persuade the heart. And they certainly can't explain why God does things the way He does. His ways are a mystery to us; He said so Himself. So it is that our response to such mysteries is a great indicator of the realness of our belief.

GOD IS ...

> I would rather live in a world where my life is sur-
> rounded by mystery than live in a world so small
> that my mind could comprehend it.[1]
>
> —Harry Emerson Fosdick

God is infinite. Let that sink in for a second. *Infinite.* It's a word we apply to almost nothing, at least not without hyperbole, because this world and everything in it are finite. Everything has limits. Everything has borders. Everything has a time span. Everything dies or decays. Everything, if given enough time, can be deconstructed, explained, and understood by someone. Not God.

God is *perfect.* This is a term we use often, but rarely in the correct sense. We call our lovers perfect. We call a date or a vacation perfect. We call a school or a job a perfect fit. Truly, though, nothing is perfect. We know this; everything has flaws. Everything is lacking in some way. Everything can be improved. Except God.

God is good. He is not good like Mr. Rogers or Mother Teresa. He is not a decent fellow or a good man. He is not good like the time you had at the movies or like LeBron James is at basketball. God is the very essence of good. Everything good in the world, whether moral or beautiful or skillful or enjoyable, is a reflection of God. To say God is good is not like saying the floor is wet. It is more like saying water is wet (although even that falls short of capturing the intertwining of God and good).

HOW DO WE KNOW?

Answering the question of how we know that God is infinite, perfect, and good is one of the greatest tasks of Christianity. So many of those who refuse to commit their lives to God do so because they do not see God this way. In fact, most of the world, especially the Western world, doesn't see Him this way.

The enlightened, progressive world, if they believe in God at all, sees Him as subservient to their understanding and human rules of logic, justice, fairness, and morality. They don't think too much about where standards of logic, justice, fairness, and morality come from. In short, they submit God to their wills and whims. If He does not abide by their framework of understanding, He either is not good or does not exist. So Christians are burdened to answer questions about God's infinite existence and His perfect and good nature.

Can we prove that He is so? No. We can't even prove God exists. We can give evidence and arguments from Scripture, but evidence and argumentation are incomplete. We can provide philosophical arguments and even some scientific indications. But people's souls don't work like a court of law where a preponderance of evidence can sway a jury. A good closing argument in a discussion about the character of God will not win the day. A friend once told me a story of a conversation he had with his brother who did not believe in God. They stayed up late into the night shooting pool in their parents' basement and arguing about the existence and character of God. As the sun rose, his brother dropped his pool cue on the table and said, "Look, I hear everything you're saying, and it all makes sense. But I just don't believe." Then he walked up the stairs and went to bed. Evidence can convince the intellect of certain facts, but it cannot sway the soul past the point of "I just don't believe."

Sharing our experiences, telling our stories (or "testimonies" as church folks like to call them), helps to close the gap. Explaining how we feel about God and how we came to feel that way is an effective approach to use to connect with people. Sharing how we've seen His goodness and marveled at His bigness gives some humanity and personal connection to big concepts. But at the same time experience is easily discounted. I know plenty of people who have had great experiences at restaurants or concerts, whereas my experiences in the same situations were less than stellar. One person's experience often has little bearing on another's.

So many Christians struggle to explain how we know of God's character and essence. One group leans too heavily on a CSI method: collect evidence, analyze it, and provide proof. Another group treats experiential evidence as enough, as if what they've experienced is the recipe for every other person's belief. What is missing is this: relationship.

In the previous chapter, I wrote of knowing someone in relationship versus knowing a lot about someone. Only in relationship do you know the essence of someone's character. You know through connecting with them. The same is true with God.

When we are in relationship with God, His Word becomes more than a book; it becomes alive. It becomes personal. We often read the Bible like a textbook, looking for the basic information. Others read it like a *Chicken Soup for the Soul* sort of inspirational boost (they must skip pretty much the whole Old Testament). Many others read through it as a storybook of disparate tales offering morals and lessons like Aesop's fables do. But if we are in relationship with God, we begin to see it is a *revelation*. It is a window into who God is, one that He gave us to share exactly what we need to know of Him.

I learned this through Wayne Martindale, a former professor of mine at Wheaton College and an elder at the church I attended at the time. He was walking with me through a hard time, and we were discussing my dry spiritual state. I was at a place where I felt I didn't even know how to read the Bible in a useful way. I had a theology degree, had led ministries, and had read the entire Bible at least a half dozen times, but here I was, empty. Dr. Martindale is a literature professor, so he knows reading. He knows how to parse and explicate and draw out themes. He is a gifted teacher. But he didn't give me any techniques. He simply told me to start reading the Gospels and get to know Jesus. Look for who the real Jesus is. He recognized that what I was missing in all my familiarity with

Scripture was a personal, powerful connection to Jesus Christ—the living Word. His advice made all the difference. It didn't happen quickly. But like a bucket being filled by a dripping faucet, I found myself getting filled up with a real Jesus, one I hadn't known before. I read the Word and met the Word.

When something like this happens, no longer is the Bible just a lengthy book of many words; it is alive. It speaks. And it reads us as we read it.

> For the word of God is living and active, sharper
> than any two-edged sword, piercing to the division
> of soul and of spirit, of joints and of marrow, and
> discerning the thoughts and intentions of the heart.
> —Hebrews 4:12

As we see the Bible come alive, God's character becomes clear. Before relationship with God, the Bible's declarations of God are statements to be weighed and tested. Once in relationship with Him, they are promises that can be trusted.

> What, now, is faith? Nothing other than the cer-
> tainty that what God says is true.[2]
> —Andrew Murray

Relationship with God is how we know His attributes, His character. Just as it is how we know anyone else's. Through relationship we learn that we can trust aspects of God we can't see or understand. He proves Himself to us; we know Him. Just as we don't doubt our closest friends when they aren't with us and we trust a doctor to do a surgery we ourselves cannot do, so we learn to trust God when we cannot see Him or understand His actions. Only far more so! Friends fail us and doctors make mistakes, yet we still trust them. But being in relationship with God allows us to see that He will never fail us or screw up.

Just as we can only know God's essence in relationship with Him, so too the rest of the world can only see it through our relationships with Him. People get to know of my wife because I speak of her, describe what makes her tick, and explain her character. But people begin to understand her when they see her relate to me and to our daughters. Just so, people will see God for who He is through our relationships with Him. What separates Him from any human relationship, though, is infinite, perfect relational capacity. There are no limits to whom God can relate with. Even that is evidence of His character.

WHAT WE CAN'T KNOW

One of the most significant aspects of our relationship with God is how it anchors us in all the things we cannot know or understand. And there is much we cannot know. By "cannot," I don't mean we are prohibited from knowing it but that we are incapable of knowing it.

Something infinite, by definition, cannot be understood completely by someone finite. Despite man's best efforts to refute this (by action if not reason), it remains true. The finite lives within the infinite and cannot grasp the extent of it because the infinite has no extent at all. We can grasp only those things that have limits. Trying to understand the infinite is like trying to reach the end of a road that has no end; it isn't even logically feasible. God's infinity stretches endlessly beyond your or my capacity to understand it. His infinite power (omnipotence), infinite knowledge (omniscience), and infinite presence (omnipresence) are things we can speak of but not fully understand. That's what makes Him God!

Our imperfections have undermined our capacity to connect with God in certain ways because He is perfect. Every action, every thought, every plan of God is perfect. We are unable even to imagine what perfect motives, a perfect plan, and perfect knowledge of all things past, present, and future even mean. We have never encountered perfection anywhere, so we are inclined to mistrust it in God. God is holy; that is, He is *other*. His perfection puts Him on an entirely different plane from us, but because He is so different, so outside our experience and ability to understand, we mistrust Him. Rather than looking at His holiness as a mark of perfect trustworthiness, we think so highly of ourselves as if to say "Well, I don't get it, so it can't be good" whenever He does something we can't fathom.

> Faith is deliberate confidence in the character of God whose ways you may not understand at the time.[3]
>
> —Oswald Chambers

This world is fallen. Sin has tainted everything. I was born a sinner. From day one if you told me not to do something, that was the very thing I had in my head to do: run into the street, climb that fence, touch that outlet, eat that cookie. My children were born sinners. At two years old they each gained the nickname "Terrible" for a reason, and nobody had taught them to be that way. When my wife or I would reprimand them, both would do the same thing: arch their backs; get big, wide eyes; and flex every muscle in their bodies while their faces turned beet red. The pose would have been hilariously cute if it hadn't been done in outright defiance. It was as if the word *no* caused a severe physical reaction (unless of course they said it; then it was great fun, and the louder the better). Nobody had taught them that or made them act that way. It was just in them from birth. And it's in you, too; you were born a sinner. So we know nothing of pure, unadulterated *goodness*. We know good as a partial trait of some things but not as the essence of a being. Even those people we call "good," the best men and women we know, do bad and are capable of great evil. God does no bad and is capable of no evil.

Each one of these traits is impossible to get our minds around. Combined into a single being, they are beyond any comprehension. This means that the vast majority of what God does is outside of our ability to explain. We *cannot* explain how or why God does so many things. We cannot explain how an omnipotent, good God brings about evil without being evil Himself. Somehow evil is evil even when it fits into the perfect plan of an all-powerful, all-good God. It is a mystery. Just not the nice, neat, fun kind.

CULTURE'S RESPONSE TO MYSTERY

We live in a "prove it" culture, dating back several centuries. Once upon a time the supernatural was recognized as just as real as the natural, and spiritual forces were just as valid as physical ones. In much of the world this still holds true today, but not in the West. Enlightenment thinking brought with it a mind-set that man is central, the highest life-form. The fallout of that is that god (not God) is whatever people want him or it to be. And for many, it means that God does not exist. They see the lack of empirical evidence for God to be proof that He does not exist.

The argument against God's existence is the most extreme response to mystery. Because the biggest questions of why and how cannot be answered clearly, the assumption is that no God exists to answer them. The world has evolved to where it is, there is little purpose to our being, and when life ends, it ends completely. Many atheists came to that point of view through pain and suffering. They saw no rhyme or reason for them and could not reconcile them with a good and loving God, so their conclusion was that God simply could not exist.

> Faith is the great cop-out, the great excuse to evade
> the need to think and evaluate evidence. Faith is
> belief in spite of, even perhaps because of, the lack
> of evidence.[4]
>
> —Richard Dawkins

This response to the mystery of why leaves the asker no more satisfied than if there were a God he or she simply couldn't understand. It plainly says that mystery exists because mystery exists—in this case the mystery of pain and suffering. Atheists find it satisfactory, at least to a degree, to have "eliminated" one source of mystery because it doesn't fit their framework of the world. By their definition of "good" and in their understanding of "powerful," a God who allows for or brings about pain cannot be a good God. Therefore He cannot exist. The end.

Such a framework that God has to fit into will inherently limit Him. It demands that He make sense to us, and if He doesn't, it is He who must change, not us. Most people don't outright eliminate God; they simply diminish Him. Some view Him as lacking power—God is not omnipotent. Some view Him as distant—He kick-started the world and now lets it run on its own. This is a belief similar to Deism.[5] While most Christians would not espouse it, for many, their lives indicate they are functional Deists. They believe in the existence of God but not in His power or participation in daily life. In fact, most of us fall into this.

In the movie *The Usual Suspects*, Kevin Spacey's character, "Verbal" Kint, says one of the great lines in recent movie history: "The greatest trick the devil ever pulled was convincing the world he didn't exist." While this is true, equally as true is the ease with which we forget God exists. We go through life as lords of our own little universes, solving problems with our own abilities and strengths and depending on external circumstances or therapies to massage our moods. We forget God until we are at wit's end; then we cry out for help. We don't need Him at work. We don't need Him at school. We don't need Him anywhere. Until we do. Then we seek to summon Him from on high or wherever it is that He waits until we beckon. We live most days as if we appreciate God's good work in making the world and are glad He went home when He was finished, kind of like the contractor who built the addition on your house.

When we aren't forgetting God, we're often trying to release Him from responsibility for things we don't understand by diminishing His knowledge of events or ability to impose Himself on the choices of people. Some theologians have questioned God's foreknowledge, His ability to know what will happen in the future; because if He has that, it must mean He has determined the future, which would take away human free will. On a more personal level we often emphasize the evil of a person or the randomness of nature when tragedy strikes, and we ignore, intentionally or otherwise, the fact that God is omnipotent and that He Himself says, "I make well-being and create calamity."[6]

Of course, none of our frameworks for God have any actual bearing on who He is. Each simply represents a framework, a box, into which people fit God to make themselves feel better about who He is.

Ultimately, these frameworks stem from hearts that cannot abide submitting to someone else as all-powerful. To do so would mean relinquishing control of their own lives and, just as difficult, their understanding of the world. If I believe that I am the most important being in the world, I will create a system into which the world fits and that suits my sensibilities. As a finite person, I will shrink the world to fit my finitude. And that most definitely excludes an infinite God.

CHRISTIANS' RESPONSE TO MYSTERY

Christians fall prey to this kind of thinking as frequently as non-Christians do. We live in a milieu in which it is utterly countercultural to believe in a God who is beyond our understanding and explanation. Unanswerable mysteries eat at Christians as much as they do everyone. Such questions are the reason many Christians leave the faith. They simply cannot reconcile what they don't understand about God with what they see in the world around them.

You can observe it at any public university: A good church kid comes into a religion course and immediately has his fragile belief challenged by a professor. His faith crumbles. The unanswerable outweighs the answers he has at his disposal. I even saw this at my Christian college as students were exposed to various philosophers or scientists. The mysteries overwhelmed them, and some were not able to see God through them.

Whether it is a result of the same Enlightenment thinking that pushed the broader culture to marginalize God, a fear of having our belief system challenged from within, or something else, the church has largely suppressed mystery and the discussion of it. Just as the broader culture has created frameworks to limit God, the church has created them to "justify" Him, as if He needs our help giving reasons for Himself.

Take the difficult question of why bad things happen if God is good and all-powerful. Some traditions teach that all the hard things in the world happen as a judgment for sin. Most don't go that far but do say that every bad thing that happens is a result of sin's sabotaging of people and creation. Some are very bold to say that tragedies, especially natural ones, are the hand of God at work. Others skirt the issue and emphasize God's care for victims instead (which really offers no answer to the question of why bad things happen). Each of these falls short of satisfactory, though. If every tragedy is a judgment for sin, then why don't all sins of the same type bring about the same tragedy and some sins not result in any tragedy at all? If God is the hand behind every tragedy, how can He also care for the victims? If He cares only for the victims, who's in charge of the tragedies? The questions are myriad, and this is referencing just one flavor of mystery.

Simply put, the church is not comfortable presenting an answer of "We don't know." The church is where people expect to find answers; so in many cases answers have been fabricated to appease the askers. We have followed the tradition of Job's friends. They tied his suffering to the sin they assumed he had committed because that was a framework, a cause and effect they could understand. While we in the church may not commit that exact same error, we do make others. One of our greatest is the misuse of God's promises. We treat them as magic pills to make all the badness go away. We seek to claim them and apply them as we see fit. But they aren't our promises; they're God's. He will keep them, for certain, but not in the time frame we may want or with the application we feel we need. We have sought to come up with nicely organized answers to questions that simply have no satisfactory answers, at least not to the average questioner. Just as people are unwilling to not have an answer, the church is unwilling to not give one.[7]

THE BIBLE'S RESPONSE TO MYSTERY

The book of Job is built around the question why. God allowed Satan to take Job's possessions, kill his children, and strike him ill. The first thirty-seven chapters of the book are a discourse between Job and three of his friends. They insisted, based on their framework for God, that Job was being punished for sinning. All he had to do was admit his sin and repent, and God would restore him, because, they explained, God was a just God. They had a high view of God's sovereignty and His justice and even His mercy. But they had confined Him to a system they could understand: every calamity was the punishment for a sin, so therefore, every calamity had a simple resolution—repent and make restitution. Job protested that he was innocent, and the beginning of the book reveals that Job was indeed a righteous man. He rejected his friends' theories and pleaded his case before God instead.

Here we are introduced to a series of questions. Why did God allow all the tragedies? What does it mean about God's character that He allowed them? Since God allowed Satan to act, He clearly could have stopped it (in fact, He gave Satan clear limitations on what he could do); so why didn't He?

And God answered these questions. In chapter 38, He responded to Job. But they were not the answers Job was looking for, nor were they the answers we as readers expected. Rather than explaining His actions, God turned the questions back on Job. He described His power and magnificence in this blistering sequence of queries. He asked Job if he had been present when the world was created. Had he breathed life into the animals or fed the infants? Did he make the seasons happen? Here is how God began:

Then the LORD answered Job out of the whirlwind
and said:

"Who is this that darkens counsel by words
without knowledge?

Dress for action like a man;
> I will question you, and you make it known
>> to me.

"Where were you when I laid the foundation of
>> the earth?
> Tell me, if you have understanding.
Who determined its measurements—surely you
>> know!
> Or who stretched the line upon it?
On what were its bases sunk,
> or who laid its cornerstone,
when the morning stars sang together
> and all the sons of God shouted for joy?

"Or who shut in the sea with doors
> when it burst out from the womb,
when I made clouds its garment
> and thick darkness its swaddling band,
and prescribed limits for it
> and set bars and doors,
and said, 'Thus far shall you come, and no farther,
> and here shall your proud waves be stayed'?

"Have you commanded the morning since your
>> days began,
> and caused the dawn to know its place …?"[8]

For five chapters God relentlessly questioned Job, blistered him, and left him with no response but a clear sense of just how much bigger God was than his understanding.

Job's simple reply was "I am unworthy—how can I reply to you? I put my hand over my mouth."[9] This is the least modern, least American reply imaginable. Unworthy? Humble silence? Express yourself, man! Make your case! No. Job got it right. He saw who God was, or rather he saw *enough* of who God was, to realize that God was and forever will be the infinite, omnipotent, perfect deity who acts rightly even if His methods are beyond the scope of human understanding.

You know what the book of Job doesn't do? It doesn't explain *anything*. But even without explanations or rationales it does answer our questions. God is *God*. We are not. Be silent.

> Where reason cannot wade, there faith may swim.[10]
> —Thomas Watson

The question of God's election is one of the more hotly debated and most mysterious doctrinal questions in Scripture. Do we choose God, or does He choose us? If He chooses us, then why are those who are not chosen held responsible for not being saved? Why do they go to hell if He didn't choose them to be saved? Is a God who condemns those He chose not to save an unjust God? Romans 9 puts forth answers to these questions. In it Paul posed the question of why God saves some people (specifically Jews) and not others. Verses 14–18 explain it this way:

What shall we say then? Is there injustice on God's part? By no means! For he says to Moses, "I will have mercy on whom I have mercy, and I will have compassion on whom I have compassion." So then it depends not on human will or exertion, but on God, who has mercy. For the Scripture says to Pharaoh, "For this very purpose I have raised you up, that I might show my power in you, and that my name might be proclaimed in all the earth." So then he has mercy on whomever he wills, and he hardens whomever he wills.

As in Job the answer is not the one we came looking for. It doesn't tell me how it works or why God does it this way. It simply tells me God does it this way and because He is God He is rightly just and rightly merciful. Does that make sense to me? No, not really at all. Should it? I don't think so.

Paul went on to answer the other pressing questions in verses 19–23.

You will say to me then, "Why does he still find fault? For who can resist his will?" But who are you, O man, to answer back to God? Will what is molded say to its molder, "Why have you made me like this?" Has the potter no right over the clay, to make out of the same lump one vessel for honorable use and another for dishonorable use? What if God, desiring to show his wrath and to

> make known his power, has endured with much
> patience vessels of wrath prepared for destruction,
> in order to make known the riches of his glory
> for vessels of mercy, which he has prepared before-
> hand for glory ...?

God is the potter. We are the clay. As a kid I grew up singing a song about that in youth group, but I never thought about the implications. God can do what He will with me. And with you. He could have decided not to create us. He could have decided to bring me into a family in China or Alaska or Chile. He could have made me anything He wanted to because He made me from nothing. I wasn't anything before God acted and I became a living organism—not a thought, a prayer, or a gleam in my mother's eye. He is the infinite, perfect, good potter. I am the finite, imperfect lump of soil.

What is more, my understanding of God is akin to a pile of clay's understanding of the potter. It's not just that He has the power and I don't; it's that as a created being I simply cannot fathom who He is or what He is doing aside from what He cares to reveal to me. I want to think of myself as something powerful and amazing. He made me unique, with talents and abilities. I reflect Him to the world. But next to God I am simply clay and He is the One at the wheel, spinning, crafting, making. This is the hardest reality in the world for me to swallow, to come to grips with. I am at the mercy of God and cannot know what He will do—it's not that I am not allowed to but rather that I am unable. I hate that. And I need it.

Scripture doesn't offer the answers to most mysteries that we want. It offers the ones God wants us to have. And if He wants us to have them, then they are the ones we need. This is not an easy truth because it does not *feel* satisfying. But satisfaction is there to be had.

LIVING IN MYSTERY

Satisfaction can be found in God. Relationship with Him provides our souls the confirmations we need to fill in the spaces our minds can't fill. Know God deeply and you will find His goodness overwhelming. Dwell with Him and while you won't stop having questions, you will find the peace to live with them, knowing that God's character is immutably good. His love is unchanging and unending. Just as Scripture presents us with mysteries and bitter medicine to swallow, it offers us promises of God's character that are the sugar with which we take that medicine. Psalm 136 says:

> Give thanks to the LORD, for he is good,
>> for his steadfast love endures forever.
> Give thanks to the God of gods,
>> for his steadfast love endures forever.
> Give thanks to the Lord of lords,
>> for his steadfast love endures forever;
>
> to him who alone does great wonders,
>> for his steadfast love endures forever;
> to him who by understanding made the heavens,
>> for his steadfast love endures forever;
> to him who spread out the earth above the waters,
>> for his steadfast love endures forever;

> to him who made the great lights,
>> for his steadfast love endures forever;
> the sun to rule over the day,
>> for his steadfast love endures forever;
> the moon and stars to rule over the night,
>> for his steadfast love endures forever.[11]

In this passage, we can see parallels to the relentless questioning of Job. The psalmist described the same power that God did in the book of Job—the power over the heavens and the earth and the sea. But with every action comes the promise: His steadfast love endures forever. In Job, the power was used to show the distance between God and man, but here it was used to show the closeness. In Job, it put us humans in our place, but here it showed that our place is close to God, safe in His care. Just as a man can use a strong arm to fight, he can also use it to embrace; he can use it to wield a hammer or hold his child's hand. So it is with God except instead of a strong arm He has infinite power and infinite care. His steadfast love endures through all mystery; no matter how much the questions eat at us, His steadfast love endures forever. It endures through all pain; no matter who stabs us in the back or betrays us, no matter what consequences we face for our actions, His steadfast love endures forever.

We cannot drive God's love away with our badness. In fact, the greatest sign of His steadfast love is the very means of paying for our badness and doing away with it—Jesus Christ. I have never known God's steadfast love more than when I have been at my most ashamed, most broken, most certain He was done with me. But there I saw it, the steadfast love of forgiveness and grace. His steadfast love endures, period. We are given mystery and promise in the same revelation. They are both true. So long as we are in relationship with God we live in both.

To be true believers we must come to the place of uncomfortable comfort. In this life we will never be settled. Every time a tragedy happens, we will ask why and an answer likely won't be readily available. Every time a friend or loved one makes self-destructive decisions and rejects the hope of the gospel, we will ask when and how. And we might be greeted with silence. This is the uncomfortable part. The comfort comes from drawing close to God, through His Word, and seeing the parts of Himself He has chosen to reveal. In those parts, those glimpses He has given through Scripture, we have enough to be comforted as we live lives surrounded by mystery.

Chapter 4

A PRAYER FROM WHERE?

"I believe; help my unbelief." The prayer of the father in Mark 9 is the banner over all of these questions, this mystery, this exploring, this examination of God and belief. It is the spark that ignited these thoughts for me, but it is more than that. It is a theme of life. It represents where my faith comes from and the place where it is going.

To explain what I mean by where my faith originates, let's revisit the father in Mark 9. Did he come to Jesus out of desperation? Absolutely. But in order to come at all he had to believe at least a little bit. Something he had heard about Christ stuck in his craw; he couldn't get rid of it. Something made Jesus seem better than the phonies and the fake healers who paraded their services around. Maybe it was the sheer number of people proclaiming all the miracles Jesus had done. Maybe it was because he had heard specifically of Jesus handling His business with demons. Something made the father believe enough to take an action step, a step of faith.

"I believe; help my unbelief" is more than a statement; it is a request. It is a request *to* someone. Requests can stem only from belief, even if it is just the tiniest inkling of belief. I don't send letters to Santa asking for Christmas presents because I don't have any inkling of belief he exists. If one of my teeth were knocked out, I wouldn't leave it under my pillow hoping for a cash reward from the tooth fairy; I don't believe she exists. To request—to pray—as the father did shows a modicum of belief that the request can be granted.

And his belief can be seen not just in the fact that he prayed but also in *what* he prayed. He asked for help to believe more, to believe better. He saw his unbelief and knew it was a hindrance. Such a request can only come from a starting point of belief. A dead person can't ask a doctor to make her well; there must be life in her to do that. So it is with the prayer to "help my unbelief." A speck of belief must be present to pray at all. You might think, *Well, of course the father believed; he said so himself.* But his words did not substantiate much of anything. It was his actions of faith and his plea for greater belief that proved his words.

ASKING FOR HELP

As someone who grew up in the church and sat under rigorous Bible teaching, I have been subjected to perpetual guilt about the lack of fervor in my belief. At every turn—youth camps, sermons, missions trips, small groups—there was the constant reminder that I did not believe as I ought to, that my faith was too small and too weak. Added to that was the emptiness caused by my own misconception of belief growing up. I genuinely wanted to live a life that was honoring to God, but my relationship with Him was ill formed and underdeveloped, so I couldn't. I knew so much of Him but did not know Him intimately.

I swung back and forth between extreme confidence in my standing with God, an "I'm all good" mentality, and a vacuous heart that felt little and was often prone to sin. When I was feeling good toward God, I was king of the spiritual world, and when I fell into sin, whether or not anyone knew of it (usually not), I felt crushed, a failure. I wanted the elation of belief as I knew it but struggled to pray, "Help my unbelief."

In fact, I struggled to ask anyone for help with anything. Between pride and insecurity I could not admit to not knowing or not being able. I avoided circumstances that would expose an inability to do things, even certain sports or social situations. One of my greatest fears was looking like a fool. Asking for help didn't feel like a positive thing; it felt humiliating. I couldn't ask anyone for help with anything, so I definitely couldn't humble myself to ask God, "Help my unbelief." As a result, my faith faltered and sin ate up my life from the inside out. I rationalized, I segmented my life, and I kept up the veneer of belief, but my facade was thinning and weakening as I became more caught up in sin over the years. My unbelief kept me from asking for help from God or His people to believe more.

In the end, what opened my eyes was the humbling I needed, although it was more like humiliation. I was fired from my job for dishonest dealings. It was a job I was good at and enjoyed, working for people I respected greatly. My wife had no awareness of any of it and was stunned; the man she had trusted and thought of as a paragon of virtue had fallen far short of her expectations. She questioned everything about me. Was I really who she thought? The answer was yes and no. I wasn't as good as she thought. I had lied and kept secrets. Neither was I a false front of an evil monster. I loved my family, my church, and even my God. I just loved myself more.

In chapter 2, I wrote of how years before this firing, my mentor, Mark, had challenged my mental assent to the ways of God and prodded me toward a real belief. But even as he nudged me, I merely mentally assented to his point, continuing the same pattern of knowing the right answers and not letting them change me. But now I was faced with the question, did I believe or not? If I did not believe, the easiest actions would have been to walk away and to avoid the pain of confession, of rebuilding lost trust, of putting myself at the mercy of church leaders, and especially of seeking restoration with my wife.

But I did believe. Getting fired, having my long-hidden pattern of sin exposed, was a relief even as it was excruciating. God was creating an opportunity for me to get past my obstacles of pride and insecurity, the ones that had nourished so much of my sin, and finally say, "Help my unbelief." And I was able to do so. I was able to get help from our church's leaders, who both pushed me and guided me. I was able to get help from close friends who walked through the door of my vulnerability to ask questions I never would have let them ask previously and invest in my soul. And I was able to be honest with my wife. None of this was easy. It took months and months of "restorative therapy" for my soul. It was similar to having a knee reconstructed and going through therapy to regain the ability to stand, and then stumbling, walking, and finally running. Except that in this case I wasn't *re*gaining health; I was finding it for the first time.

It was during this process that I encountered the power of the father's prayer from Mark 9. Being a good little Christian boy I had read this passage a hundred times, but one day I read it again and stopped. Then I read it one more time. That's when I realized it was reading me, speaking to me. I was fixated on that sentence: "I believe; help my unbelief." It spoke of everything I had been through and was pursuing. It spoke of the desire of my heart and the direction of my life.

I saw for the first time that the starting point of asking for help is belief, just as the father was drawn to Jesus by some inkling of belief. I saw the ongoing tension, even for Christians, of believing enough to look to God for help to overcome the unbelief that is defeating us. I saw my own decades of inability to really pray this prayer because I was afraid to submit to the help of God. But now that God had reached down and forcibly helped me, I saw that, scary as it might be, pleading "Help" is a God-honoring act of faith.

"HELP": A CRY OF BELIEF

> "Lord, I believe; help my unbelief" is the best any
> of us can do really, but thank God it is enough.[1]
> —Frederick Buechner

If you are a Christian, you believe, but there are times when all you can say is "Help my unbelief." You feel nothing for Jesus. You have no passion, no desire to follow. You are helpless to kick-start your heart. It all seems vain. So you grumble or gasp out that short prayer of desperation.

You are stuck between your belief—you know God exists and that He is good and loves you—and your unbelief. Under all this, for those with true faith, is an object of our belief—God Himself. So no matter how difficult things get, how dry your soul feels, how broken down you are, you can look to God and pray, "Help my unbelief." It feels like an admission of guilt, like a statement of failure, but here is what's remarkable about that prayer: to pray it at all is to announce, "I believe." We cannot pray that prayer unless we do believe!

If you have cried out to God, "Help," you have spoken from a place of belief. That is evidence of your faith. You may not feel it, but your actions are showing it. Of course you need help; you're a sinner, after all. But do not fall into despair so long as you can look toward God and ask, "Help."

A PRAYER FOR AN "ALREADY, BUT NOT YET" LIFE

It's cheaper to drive on long trips with two children than it is to fly, so that's how my family usually travels. Inevitably, about an hour into an eight-hour drive, one of our daughters asks, "Are we there yet?" It's as if kids don't notice that we're driving freeway speeds with no sign of stopping. Christians live "Are we there yet?" lives. In its entirety, life is a state of traveling toward a destination. We are pursuing holiness and growth. We are seeking to become more like Christ, to live lives that reflect and honor God. But we live in a fallen state marked by sin. It often feels as if we are spinning our wheels rather than making progress, the same way children feel in the backseat. The progress we do see is often three steps forward, two and a half steps back. We are never "there." We don't arrive.

And yet we have arrived. Our hope is certain through the promise of God given in Jesus. It is a promise of the Holy Spirit, ever present in believers to guide and to grow and to mature them. It is a promise of salvation, of eternal life, of a new heaven and a new earth coming one day. It is not here yet, but it is certain because we know God's promises are unbreakable and utterly reliable. It is certain because He sent His Son, His beloved Son, to die so that we could have this hope. God will not waste the death of His Son. This much is certain and complete.

Theologians often talk about the "already, but not yet" state of the world. We have already received salvation but not yet fully realized it. We have already been given a promise that is certain but not yet seen it come to fruition. We have already seen Jesus bring God's kingdom to earth but not yet seen His kingdom in all its glory and perfection. If this seems like a bunch of theoretical, high-minded stuff, then think of it in this context: your life is an "already, but not yet" life.

You are saved, but you are not perfectly holy. You trust Jesus, but you do not follow Him perfectly. You want to serve Him well, but you fall short. You are in relationship with God, but you wander and seek other gods. You have submitted to God, but you often try to be your own god. You believe, but you battle unbelief.

"I believe; help my unbelief" should be the daily cry of every Christian. It is the cry of someone in the depths of despair who has only enough belief to say that prayer. And it is the cry of the fire-filled preacher before standing in the pulpit on Sunday morning. It is the cry of the mother who is running out of patience with her children and the businessman who is just a couple of clicks away from viewing porn. It is the cry of the person who is spiritually dry and has no desire to open her Bible and the person who has devoured all of Romans and is starting on 1 Corinthians just this morning. It is the cry of the sinner caught in an affair who deeply yearns to repent, to leave behind his shameful ways and be whole in Jesus and in marriage. It is a confession of need. It is a celebration of hope. It is the full scope of a life of faith.

At no point in this life will we believe perfectly, so we will need this prayer until the day Jesus makes our souls whole, removes our sin, and gives us perfect belief upon His return. Or we may die first, but then we will enter the presence of God and His holiness will burn away our unbelief until all that is left is Christ's righteousness in us, sinless belief. Every time we pray it we can take heart because it is a signet of faith, a mark of a true believer. Because the desire to believe can stem only from belief.

Chapter 5

UNBELIEF AND DOUBT

Christianity has done its utmost to close the circle and declared even doubt to be sin. One is supposed to be cast into belief without reason, by a miracle, and from then on to swim in it as in the brightest and least ambiguous of elements: even a glance towards land, even the thought that one perhaps exists for something else as well as swimming, even the slightest impulse of our amphibious nature—is sin![1]

—Friedrich Nietzsche

For many who are from traditional evangelical contexts, the idea of a Christian not believing is anathema. They will feel their consciences condemning them for even considering it. The general expectation, not always expressed but always felt, is that good, solid Christians have no doubts and can defend or explain everything they believe. The idea of exploring our unbelief is terrifying, and many won't even go there. That realm of doubt and grays and fog is where the wild things are. It's much safer to stay in a nicely organized, easily explained, strongly fortified world of belief.

What happens, though, when unbelief breaks in? What happens when doubts and questions break through the walls of their comfy domestic belief? The wild things wreak havoc. They destroy the flimsy arguments life is built on. It is more dangerous to live in a safe little world refusing to acknowledge the wild, scary world of unbelief than it is to prepare well and engage it. And we, the church, families, don't do a good job of preparing our kids to handle the questions.

Instead, we do a great job of teaching them to listen to figures of authority without questions. "The pastor said it, I believe it, that settles it." Until the college professor contradicts the pastor and tears his argument to shreds. What then? Then the wild things of doubt and unbelief tear the kid apart from the inside out. What happens when we build our lives on comfort, domestic bliss, and collecting "blessings" from God but then loss of employment happens, divorce happens, destitution happens, or disease happens? Then the wild things rip that false faith to shreds and scatter the pieces far and wide.

This is why we must begin engaging the wild things, the questions, the doubts and teach our kids to do the same, bit by bit, as they mature. Engaging may leave you bruised and battered, but naively waiting for the doubts to come get you could leave your faith mangled and permanently maimed. How, some ask, is it better to deal in doubts and fears than to rest in peaceful oblivion? Because until those things are defeated they will always pose a threat. That bucolic existence will be under constant threat unless the wild things are beaten back.

UNBELIEVING DOUBT

Doubt is a powerful and mysterious force. It is built mostly on questions, but those stem from a huge range of human realities: fear, anger, logic, intuition, and observation, to name a few. Because of these complexities, doubt can be either motivating or enervating. It can cripple or it can restore. Unbelieving doubt is that which cripples.

In the previous chapter, I wrote about the "already, but not yet" state of Christianity. The unbelieving sort of doubt stops a person from moving forward. If this life is a journey toward the "not yet," then this sort of doubt stops progress cold. It is the sort of doubt that looks ahead at what God promises and says either "I don't think I want that" or "I don't believe that exists." It is rebellion.

When unbelieving doubt poses a question, it is not interested in the answer for any reason other than to disprove it. Unbelieving doubt is on the attack. It is much more interested in the devastating effect of the question itself to erode the asker's belief and hope in what is being questioned. The asker is not asking to learn; she is asking in order to devastate. She does not want to progress to an answer. She wants to show that there is no answer. Unbelieving doubt is not working toward anything but merely against belief. These doubts are the wild monsters that wreck faith and destroy the simplistically peaceful Christian lives so many people try to lead. Friedrich Nietzsche, Christopher Hitchens, and Richard Dawkins all exemplify this sort of doubt borne out to its full extent—complete and total refusal to believe in God or His way.

BELIEVING DOUBT

It may seem like a contradiction in terms to use the phrase "believing doubt." If you believe something you do not doubt it, right? That is true only if you have full understanding of it and full confidence in it. While we ought to have full confidence in God, two things stand between us and that. First is that we cannot comprehend all that God is and what He is doing. In our culture that is reason enough to doubt, and though we saw the biblical response to such doubt, we still struggle with it. Struggle is the second obstacle. We have not arrived at a place of perfect holiness, which means we have not arrived at a place of perfect trust. We are prone to questions and doubts in spite of God's perfect goodness. It is our fallen nature.

What makes our doubt "believing doubt" is what we do with it. Unbelieving doubt is that which destroys fragile beliefs. Believing doubt is that which strengthens our beliefs. Instead of letting unbelief in, it ventures out in faith and seeks to waylay it. Just as unbelieving doubt is against belief, this sort of doubt is the driving force behind belief. It is the catalyst to find what we believe rather than the obstacle keeping us from it. It starts from the place of simple belief and becomes stronger as it encounters, engages, and overcomes unbelief. And it can do this because it is belief backed by a real, good God. It is not merely intellectual sparring, but rather spiritual engagement through the Holy Spirit.

Believing doubt will always anchor in God's character and word as unshakable and then take on questions that harass and attack. Sometimes these are emotional questions; other times they are philosophical or biblical. Sometimes they won't be answered because they are beyond the abilities of the believer or because they delve into mysteries that nobody can rightly answer. This is when the believing doubter is at his greatest risk. But if he stands fully in his relationship with God, even those unanswerable questions will not overcome him.

Doubt is not the opposite of faith; it is an element of faith.[2]

—Paul Tillich

Every mental act is composed of doubt and belief, but it is belief that is the positive, it is belief that sustains thought and holds the world together.[3]

—Søren Kierkegaard

Is it fair to call this sort of questioning doubt? Isn't *doubt* an inherently negative term? Doubt is negative when it attacks character (in this case God's character) and leads to broken relationships. But doubt can save us from much trouble and lead to much knowledge. If you see a rickety ladder, you will not climb it. You doubt its ability to hold you and thus avoid unnecessary pain. If a man in a plaid suit, with greased-back hair and a wide grin, offers to sell you "a peach of a car," you will probably doubt him; you will likely suspect the car is more of a lemon. Refusing to take culture's promises at face value and instead questioning them is a good thing. It is doubt, but doubt that seeks truth and stems from the belief that God is the source of all truth.

CHRISTIANS AND DOUBT

I have written about these two kinds of doubt in diametrically opposed terms, and that is the goal—to have a clear delineation between doubt based in belief and doubt that undermines belief. But the reality is that we waffle back and forth between the two. It is easy for me to write that believing doubt is anchored in God's perfect goodness, but to be actually anchored is not something that just happens. Sometimes we lose our anchor, not because God changes, but because we lose our hold on it.

Part of being human is being a sinner. We are rebels against God from birth. We all want to be our own gods and determine our own reality. For this reason, even believers in close relationship with God suffer from unbelieving doubt. We are prone to practice it.

Some will say they never doubt, and intellectually that may be true. Their minds may be wired not to question. But are they obedient to God? Are their lives in line with His Word? If not, then they most certainly do doubt in an unbelieving way; it is doubt in action. If belief in action is faith leading to obedience, then unbelief in action leads to disobedience whether or not the unbelief is verbally expressed or intellectually acknowledged. This describes much of my story. I did not philosophically or theologically doubt God. But my life was one of unbelief because I was doing things my way instead of His. I doubted Him at the point of decision: Would God actually give me greater joy than sin? It was unbelieving doubt in action. It wasn't until the fruit of all my unbelief became clear that I recognized its ruinous effect. I saw the hurt it caused to those around me, but what moved me was the realization that I was what kept me from God, from joy, from steadfast love. My unbelief was robbing me of what God offered, and it was collecting pain wrapped in temporal happiness.

Other Christians will fight daily battles with their intellects. I attended Wheaton College, a Christian liberal arts school in Illinois. While I was there, I had several friends who were philosophy majors, and I saw them fight and yearn and struggle to simply assent to certain realities of God. Their minds presented them with one question after another. I saw them wear down at times, feeling as if nothing could be known. I saw others come to a connection with God that saw them through the intellectual barrage. Theirs was not a struggle of disobedience first, but rather one of coming to a place of belief. Their alignment (or lack thereof) with God was a choice made based on the answers they found. Did it or did it not make sense to follow God's way?

GRACE VERSUS DOUBT

In one way or another every Christian fights unbelieving doubt. It is in our nature in this fallen world. It is a great part of the "not yet" of life. The question, though, is whether the defining characteristic of our lives is unbelieving doubt or God's grace.

A Christian who is defined by unbelieving doubt, whether intellectual or marked by lifestyle, is in a precarious position. The Bible, God's holy Word, describes how a tree is known by its fruit. If the fruit of our lives is that of questioning God at every turn with our mouths or our choices, what does that say of our roots? Are they in God? Are we tapped into His great source of grace and peace and belief?

I leave the question hanging because I cannot answer it for you. Christians, saved by grace, go through terrible times of rebellion, apathy, and other sorts of spiritual malaise. Some people oversimplify this and gauge others' salvation entirely by what can be seen in their actions or lifestyles. That simply doesn't work. Some people look like saints and have hearts full of hell (what Jesus called "whitewashed tombs"[4]). Others live like hell but are fighting internal battles back toward Jesus. Only God and the individual know where the person really is on the belief-unbelief continuum. Only God can rightly determine who is saved or unsaved. This is one of the greatest mysteries of the Christian life. God has not given us this to know.

> Fruit is always the miraculous, the created; it is never the result of willing, but always a growth. The fruit of the Spirit is a gift of God, and only he can produce it. They who bear it know as little about it as the tree knows of its fruit. They know only the power of him on whom their life depends.[5]
>
> —Dietrich Bonhoeffer

What God has put down for us in His Word are certain evidences of true belief that we can look for. The first is repentance. If I, as a believer, go through a time of unbelief, my response should be that of repentance, of turning from my sins back to belief and obedience. This isn't the same as feeling guilty or basic contrition. Those can be spurs in the side of true repentance, but by themselves they simply lead to empty apologies and false promises. "I'm so sorry; that was out of character for me. It will never happen again!" Except that it *was* part of my character. It came from inside me, and by myself I will keep acting according to that character. That is why repentance matters. Repentance looks outside one's self to Jesus and says, "I am sorry. I was wrong, and without Your help I cannot be different. Help me be different." Then, in God's grace, I set out in a different direction, away from my old self and toward a Christ-honoring life. But a person who never repents is not showing evidence of God's grace.

A second key evidence is the response of prayer. Christians who forthrightly can pray "I believe; help my unbelief" about their struggles show their need for God and a belief that He can help them. Prayer, at its most basic level, is an acknowledgment of God's reality and deity, and that is a first step toward real belief. When we reach out to God, He reaches back and makes Himself known. Our prayers build on that base to become words of thankfulness, praise, dependence, and acknowledgment that He is omnipotent and we are not. What starts as a basic "message in a bottle" becomes a rich, ongoing correspondence between a wonderful Father and a wayward, needy, dependent child. And through it the wayward becomes the faithful.

Both repentance and prayer are essential ingredients (and results) of humility, another great evidence of God's grace. They admit fault and need. They put the sinner at the mercy of others, both man and God, for forgiveness and help. Through repentance, prayer, and humility believers move away from unbelieving doubt and grow in holiness. The refusal to do these things is a spiritual red flag and evidence of wanting to be one's own god.

As long as we live in this world, we, as sinners, will doubt in both good and bad ways. We will question and wonder. If we can do so anchored in relationship with God and in the teachings of His Word, it will strengthen our belief. It will help us venture into the foggy places and fight the wild things of unbelief. If we sit back and let the doubts come to us, they will demolish our faith.

Chapter 6

BELIEF IN ACTION

Unbelieving doubt can express itself as arguments or intellectual objections to things of God. However, as I mentioned in the previous chapter, it can also express itself as disobedience to God. In fact, I think this is the most common form of unbelief—not intellectual paralysis or objection, but simple lifestyle conflict with what God commands.

When I hear the words *obedience* and *command*, my hackles rise. I dislike being told what to do. It's not that I am a troublemaker (some of my elementary school teachers and church youth leaders might disagree); I simply don't like taking orders. I like to think on my own, find my own way, and work with others to accomplish things. Hierarchical leadership bothers me. I respond well when I'm given a rationale for something, a mission, a reason for taking action—not when I am told just to do something.

My mind-set is not uncommon, especially among younger Christians. We don't respond well to authoritarianism. It's not that we dislike authority; it's that we want earned authority instead of positional authority to tell us what to do. Our respect must be earned not demanded. Even as a child I hated it when my mother would give a command, then respond to my question of "Why?" with "Because I said so." That's no sort of explanation! She clearly didn't understand. Of course, I got myself into trouble when I tried to explain that to her.

It is so hard to believe because it is so hard to obey.[1]

—Søren Kierkegaard

I run into the same sort of problem when I bring this mind-set to God's Word. It is full of commands. Some offer an explicit rationale—if you do this, you'll avoid pain and suffering—or a promise of reward. But many are put out there as "Do it." "Why?" "Because I said so, and I AM."

The emotive reaction to blunt commands is to bow up, to dig in my heels, to demand a reason. I *deserve* an explanation and the right to choose which commands are good for me. I am nobody's slave to be ordered around. Use words such as *disobey* or *rebel* all you want. I am not subservient.

This is unbelief in its rawest form.

DISOBEDIENCE AS UNBELIEF

In Genesis 3 Adam and Eve were convinced by the serpent (Satan) that they, too, were not subservient to God. They could have the knowledge that He had kept to Himself. They could choose what was best for themselves. God had simply tried to keep deity and complete knowledge from them! So, as an expression of self-confidence and an act of self-rule, they disobeyed God. And then they died. Well, they died many years later, but at the moment of disobedience death became assured. If they had followed God's way, they would have lived forever.

God's command to "eat from any tree in the garden, but not this one" was a protective measure. He was saving them from knowledge too wonderful for themselves, the knowledge of good and evil, life and death. ("Wonderful" in this case means big, powerful, and overwhelming.) Did God spell out the details of the consequence they would face? Not really. Did He warn them of what temptations might come? No. He gave them a clear command and asked that they believe in Him—that they believe His command was for their best interest. But they didn't.

Adam and Eve saw the command of God as restrictive, inhibiting, putting a limit on their happiness. It was like a fairy tale.

In Disney's movie version of *The Little Mermaid*, Ariel, a headstrong teenage mermaid, defies her father's wishes and gets close to a handsome human prince, even saving him from a storm. She falls so madly in love with him that she sells her beautiful voice to Ursula, witch of the sea, in order to become a human and try to woo the prince. If she can win the prince's heart within three days, she will regain her voice. If she can't, she will become one of Ursula's grotesque playthings. Her father tries to stop Ursula, but the agreement Ariel made is bound by stronger magic than he has.

Of course her plan backfires (being that she has no voice) as Ursula makes herself a beautiful woman and enchants the prince. Just as the prince and Ursula are about to wed and Ariel is about to become a disgusting little sea creature, a miracle rescue happens (assisted by some of Ariel's aquatic friends). She regains her voice, sings beautifully, the spell is broken, Ursula is killed, and the prince and Ariel live happily ever after.

What is less known is that this version of the story is a complete distortion of the original. In typical Disney fashion, the filmmakers took what was a pointed, stark moral lesson and made it about pursuing your dreams and romantic infatuations regardless of consequences or the wisdom of your elders. In Hans Christian Andersen's version of the story, the original version, the mermaid trades her beautiful voice with the witch for human form, but being a human is excruciatingly painful to her, like walking on knives. She dances for the prince in spite of the great pain and tries to gain his attention and everlasting love; but she loses him to another princess with whom he is actually in love. As a last resort, she is given the opportunity to kill him with an enchanted knife in order to regain her mermaid form but instead commits suicide by flinging herself from a high window. It is a rather horrific story. You can see why Disney made a few edits.

The problem is that in those edits they sanitized out the message of the story. There is an inherent promise of peace in living the life you ought, in living as you were created to be, in honoring what is good. In both versions of the story the mermaid sees her life and the command to stay away from the prince as restrictive and joy sapping. She believes happiness is with him, no matter the cost. In Disney's version she finds happiness; the deal with the devil is voided at no cost to her. In Andersen's version her deal with the devil costs the mermaid her life. Her belief in the pursuit of happiness outside of her father's wishes costs her everything. Sound familiar?

God's commands are loaded with promise. The promise is inherent in *Him.* When God says "Do not steal," He does not need to say "Because I'll give you nice things." God's "Because I said so" is a promise. When the I AM commands, He is promising the peace and relationship and connectedness and happiness that come with being in His will.

This is what Adam and Eve missed. This is what I have missed over and over and over again in my life. Disobeying the command of God is disbelieving His character. It is ignoring the inherent promise that comes from a perfect God. It is saying, "You are not infinite, you are not perfect, and while you may be good, you are not good enough." God doesn't need to earn my respect. His very existence is the qualification for my utter respect. He is not authoritarian in any petty sense of the term. He is authority itself, the essence of perfect, flawless authority. To disobey is to deny this about Him.

BELIEF AS OBEDIENCE

Faith is taking the first step, even when you don't see the whole staircase.[2]

—Martin Luther King Jr.

[To have faith in Christ] means, of course, trying to do all that He says. There would be no sense in saying you trusted a person if you would not take his advice. Thus if you have really handed yourself over to Him, it must follow that you are trying to obey Him. But trying in a new way, a less worried way. Not doing these things in order to be saved, but because He has begun to save you already. Not hoping to get to Heaven as a reward for your actions, but inevitably wanting to act in a certain way because a first faint gleam of Heaven is already inside you.[3]

—C. S. Lewis

Adam and Eve were the original unbelievers, but the Bible is also full of examples of what it looks like to obey as belief. Abraham is the prime example of this. He was commanded by God to take his family and his possessions and move to an unknown land. Yes, God made a promise to him about multiplying his lineage and making them great and blessing the world through him, but still he just up and moved, taking the word of a God who was not even the traditional god of his people. He made a massive move on faith alone. A massive move.

I know a little about moving. In the fall of 2013 I moved my family from the Chicago area to Nashville, Tennessee. We had no promises of multiplication or blessing, no visions or dreams, only a job offer and a sense it was a good move for us, and it was still hard. My wife grew up in the Chicago area, and we'd spent the first eight years of marriage there. We left behind our friends, her family, a church we loved, a good school for our daughters, and just basic familiarity. We started at zero in Tennessee—no friends, family, church, or even an idea of the best place to buy groceries. I had to use a GPS just to get to work, and we had to Google where the closest playgrounds were. My wife's Chicago accent and direct bluntness stood out like a sore thumb. We were strangers in a foreign land, and we didn't even have any cattle or sheep or servants to herd along the way. Our move had the benefits of a moving company, air-conditioned cars, and free long-distance calls. It was on faith, sure, but with the benefits of the modern world. Abraham simply acted on faith.

Later we see Abraham, this time as an old man close to ninety years old, told by God that he would have his first son. To that point

Abraham had assumed that his lineage would end, that he would pass his inheritance to a nephew or other relative. In Abraham's time and culture that was devastating, a mark of shame even. But Abraham believed, and the Bible tells us it was "credited ... to him as righteousness."[4]

Abraham's belief was more than mentally assenting to God's words. He rested in the promise and lived as if it were real. He also struggled to believe it fully, as humans are prone to do. Abraham took his wife's slave, Hagar, as a second wife, and she bore a son, Ishmael, who was not the one God had promised. Despite his missteps and doubts, Abraham shaped his life according to what God said. And God did give him a son, Isaac, when he was one hundred years old. Although Abraham's belief was imperfect and weak at times, he still took action and obeyed.

By far the most striking example of Abraham's belief as obedience came later, after his son was born. Isaac, his promised son, was the hope of his lineage and the promise of God. Until God one day told Abraham to take Isaac up to Mount Moriah and sacrifice him. That meant Abraham was to kill Isaac as an offering to God. This was a common practice with sheep, doves, or cows. It was understood that the only way to atone for guilt was to make a blood sacrifice. The death of an animal satisfied the wrath of the gods (or in this case the true God). In other cases it was a mark of worship, of honor to God. To sacrifice a child, though, was done only by some peoples who worshipped sinister, frightening gods (such as Molech). But God commanded, so Abraham set out to obey.

The rational, Western mind sees this story teetering between absurd and horrific. If God would ask such a thing, how can we rightly say He is good? That isn't good; it's sadistic. To desire the death of a child is cruelty, baseless evil. But we have no record of Abraham saying these things. We have no record of him arguing with God or resisting. The record we do have is that of Abraham stating, "God himself will provide the lamb for the burnt offering."⁵ His obedience was decidedly unhumanistic. He did not put himself above God. He did not assume he knew better than God. He did not refuse God's command because it made no sense to him. He did not abide by a created framework for the world that put God in subservience to him. He set out to obey with the firm belief that God would provide a substitute sacrifice.

When I read this story, I see a man who so understood, and believed, the character and authority of God that he could do nothing else but obey. I have no doubt he was terrified to do so, but he knew the kind of God he followed. He knew God could do no wrong. And he believed God would make a way. (Hebrews tells us that Abraham believed God would have gone so far as to resurrect Isaac if he were sacrificed; that's faith!) And God did make a way. Moments before Abraham was to kill Isaac, an angel stopped him, saying, "Now I know that you fear God, because you have not withheld from me your son, your only son."⁶ In the nearby thicket was a ram. I have to imagine the sacrifice that followed was the most profoundly celebratory and overwhelming of both Abraham's life and Isaac's life.

Hebrews 11 offers a litany of such stories from Scripture, of people who obeyed because they believed in God. They had faith. And that is what belief is. True belief looks at God and sees the extent of His character, the depths of His goodness, the profundity of His perfection, and the immensity of His power and says, "What else can I do but obey?"

All I have seen teaches me to trust the Creator for all I have not seen.[7]

—Ralph Waldo Emerson

Believing takes practice.[8]

—Madeleine L'Engle

Obedience to God will not always look logical. But God supersedes our understanding of logic. He gave us logic to help us make sense of the world, to give order to our thoughts and reasons. But logic is not greater than God. What we see as logic is an ordered way of thinking, of understanding, given to us by God. God is not illogical, but He is beyond logic. Logic applies to the finite, those things we can understand.

Obedience to God will not always feel pleasurable in the moment. The pleasures of disobedience are right there in front of us. It is more pleasurable to have sex with your girlfriend or boyfriend, to gossip, to cut someone down for laughs, to look at porn. Obedience pales in comparison to these when you are in the ecstasy and emotional high of the moment. Obedience for obedience's sake will not overcome any of these. But belief, when firmly held to and when placed in the right things, will put in front of us a reminder of the good God has for us in obedience. Obedience isn't the end; God's satisfaction in us and our pleasure in Him are. It doesn't feel tangible in the moment, but as we grow in belief, we will find it gaining power over the desire to sin. We will move on down the road toward the "not yet."

THE GAP

Doesn't that make it sound so easy? Just believe in God and your sins will fade away. Sure it takes work. Sure it will be a challenge. But over time things will steadily improve. If only.

Christians live in a gap. We give our lives to Christ, and we step into it. On the other side of the gap is glory. "Glory" may sound old-fashioned, like something a TV preacher shouted about or old hymns were sung about. I can still hear my grandfather, a traveling evangelist of the revival and crusade era, saying "Glory" with that inimitable southern preacher emphasis—"Glaw-ray!" But think of glory as you would a stunning sunset, a litter of puppies, the vastness of the Milky Way, the detail on a Monet painting, Fourth of July fireworks, crashing surf, a crescendoing symphony, or the beauty of fresh fallen snow. Each is glorious in its own way and lifts our minds and fills our hearts with … something. That something is the yearning for the perfection to come. We are not there yet. But one day Christ will bring it with Him. Revelation 21 says:

> And I heard a loud voice from the throne saying, "Look! God's dwelling place is now among the people, and he will dwell with them. They will be his people, and God himself will be with them and be their God. 'He will wipe every tear from their eyes. There will be no more death' or mourning

or crying or pain, for the old order of things has passed away."

He who was seated on the throne said, "I am making everything new!" Then he said, "Write this down, for these words are trustworthy and true."[9]

Belief does not mean sin will go away. As long as the gap exists, we cannot have that. What we can have is trajectory. True belief is that which perpetually, magnetically pulls us toward the "not yet" of Revelation 21. It finds hope when things are hard by knowing there is greater happiness, perfect happiness to come. The suffering of right now hurts, without question. Looking to the future does not deny that or shy away from it. It simply offers a way through.

When we sin, it is forward-looking belief that leads to repentance, because we know that leaving what is wrong and pursuing what is right will bring us closer to real peace and joy. We hear the call of Jesus's voice and we go toward it, which is the very nature of repentance. And it is repentance that keeps our trajectory on course, constantly nudging us back on course when we wander and yanking us back on course when we flee.

We will struggle. We will do things we know are wrong. We will battle persistent sins. But it is belief that makes us battle instead of just giving up. That porn addiction is not greater than what is to come; it may feel like it right now, but belief lifts your eyes to "making everything new." The "not yet" is a reason to fight your apathy and laziness at work. Your work may seem pointless, but it was given to you by the One who will bring in a new creation. Doesn't He want you to be part of working in His image and toward that end? Do you find yourself fighting anger or bitterness? Grace has been poured out on you and one day justice will come, so you can be filled up with grace and look forward to wrongs being righted. And as long as we are fighting, refusing to surrender our lives to sin, we are moving toward the "not yet" and even exemplifying it to the world around us.

> If I find in myself desires which nothing in this
> world can satisfy, the most probable explanation is
> that I was made for another world.[10]
>
> —C. S. Lewis

Some folks do right things without belief. Some folks claim to believe without doing right. From the outside it can be difficult to tell who believes what. In fact, it can be difficult to tell from the *inside* too. I spent a long time assuming I believed rightly, not fully realizing that my belief was hollow, missing vitality and life. I think many people who grow up Christian are the same way. They can say all the right things, answer all the questions, and do enough good to feel comfortable in their beliefs. But do they really believe? Did I? Yes and no. I was in the gap. I believed in Christ but not to the point of giving Him everything in my life.

That is the process toward the "not yet." That is the evidence of belief. Are we giving ourselves to Christ in new ways? Are we trusting parts of our lives to Him we had not previously? A relationship, a bank account, a secret sin, a secret shame, a secret pride—are we believing His goodness and authority in such a way that we offer them up?

Chapter 7

HOW DO WE BELIEVE?

After much discussion of what belief is, what it isn't, and why you should believe, the question persists: How do I believe? Maybe this should have been answered earlier, and it was in part. It just seemed more important to lay the groundwork of what and why before getting to how. Too often we emphasize pragmatism at the expense of understanding. We want seven steps to this and four key rules of that. Americans especially are wired for quick fixes and "just tell me what I need to know so I can get going." Belief doesn't work that way. Actually, most things don't work that way; those lists are shortcuts that actually truncate true effectiveness by ripping the heart and understanding out of it. That's why I waited.

And you won't find bulleted lists of ideas or numbered lists of steps to take in this book, because belief is far too alive for those. Lists work in a mechanical world, but there is no belief machine. To systematize belief would be to say that it works exactly the same for every person and in every situation. But it isn't so neat.

Belief happens in an ecosystem in which it grows organically. When a person plants a garden, she can follow all the steps—fertilize, plant, water, weed—and still plants might die, animals might eat the produce, storms might destroy the plants. All those steps help a garden grow, but God is the One who gives the growth. That's how belief works too. What about all those Christian books with neatly organized sets of instructions on how to have a more vibrant prayer life or draw closer to God or be a more godly husband? Those instructions are some authors' best efforts at putting living, organic realities into terms people can understand and implement, but they are far from the whole picture.

HOW NOT TO BELIEVE

I have written already about what belief isn't. It is not mental acknowledgment of statements about God or the Bible. That is mere mental assent and has no transformative effect on a person's life. A person cannot think himself into true belief. He can think himself into awareness and understanding, but not belief.

I have a friend named Andrew. He grew up in a church much like the one I did, heard the same kind of sermons, and sat under the same kind of Sunday school teachers. We even attended similar Christian colleges. Andrew knows all the same biblical truth I do and might even know it better because he is a voracious reader and studied philosophy and theology. When I visited Andrew a couple of years ago, we sat out on the front porch of his house on a warm summer evening and watched the city life buzz around us. We talked about faith and life, and what I heard was question after question, challenge after challenge. Andrew simply couldn't reconcile his view of the world with what he had learned about God.

Several years prior to this conversation he and his wife had lost an infant child. Their grief was not fresh, nor was it weak. How could a God who let that happen rightly call Himself good? Andrew asked. He was past the point of tears and instead sat in resigned distance and defiance. And in truth I did not have an answer for him. We knew the same things, could recite the same verses, and knew the "answers." But he did not believe them, could not believe them. He went on to question various points of theology and various attributes of God. Andrew knew what was taught about God, but he could not reconcile himself to that definition of God.

The church is also full of people who play out all the right actions without belief. Their lives are also lacking transformation, and it is the internal transformation that's missing. Their motivation is fear, pride, or self-justification instead of honoring God. I live in Tennessee, smack in the middle of the Bible Belt of the United States. Culture here is so steeped in Christianity that the public school teachers still wish people Merry Christmas and liquor stores are closed on Sundays. The downside to cultural Christianity is that the facade of morality hides the necessity for real transformation in people's hearts. When all the people around you claim to be Christian, it is difficult to convince them that their hearts need to change. They don't truly believe, but they don't rightly know the difference.

> I planted, Apollos watered, but God gave the growth.[1]
>
> —Apostle Paul

RELATIONSHIP MATTERS

The transformation of a life, internal or external, can come only in relationship with God. True belief in God *is* a relationship. In a relationship we can truly know someone else, not just know about them. The knowledge that comes in a relationship is formative. It shapes how we live. Think about your spouse or your best friend or your mom. Your relationship with each of them, your knowledge of them, has influenced your life. You act different, are aware of new things, are offended by new things, and are passionate about things all because of them.

Each of the people I just mentioned has left an imprint on you, some greater than others. If you're married, the very pattern of your daily life is shaped by your spouse—where you live, when you get up, how your weekends are spent, what you do for a job. Your spouse shapes your habits and hobbies even without trying. You live a shared life, and that means everything about you is influenced by your spouse in some way. Your mom and dad raised you and you carry their genetics. No matter what you said as a kid, you are turning into them in some ways. Your best friends speak into your life, introduce you to new experiences, and provide a rich outlet for relationship. But each of them, even your spouse, intersects with your life in just a small way compared to God.

God's connection to and intersection with your life is constant and consuming. He didn't just create you and leave you; God is the sustainer of creation. That means that every moment you exist is a moment God is keeping you in existence willfully and actively. But beyond mere existence (as if that is a "mere" anything) God gave you a soul, the everlasting being that makes you more than just a mammal. He made it unique and created it to be filled up with Him, with His Spirit. He made it to live forever with Him—if it gives itself to Him. God made us to reflect Him, to honor Him, to enjoy

Him. All that can be done only in relationship with Him. You may not entirely realize it. We tend to forget Him often. But He is there. And for that reason, relationship with God is the defining aspect of our belief in Him.

In the mid to late 1990s WWJD bracelets were all the rage, posing the question, what would Jesus do? They became so popular that they reached far beyond the realm of committed Christians. They became sort of a fashion fad and a moralistic awareness piece. But it is only in relationship with Christ that we could ever answer such a question. In the context of relationship we gain intuitions. We begin to know instinctively what actions, words, and attitudes will please Him. Just as we intuitively learn how to make our friends happy or discover what they like, so we do with God as we live in relationship with Him. Belief becomes less about calculating and more about new instincts. As in every relationship, this is an ongoing process, one in which we grow over time and through intentionality.

The more we know of the one we are in relationship with, the more opportunity there is for trust. In relationship with other people, our trust is often damaged and tested. We often damage other people's trust in us too. We are selfish sinners. No matter how much we learn of other people's desires, we still act selfishly and hurt them. But God never does. The deeper we go in relationship with Him, the greater our trust grows. Paradoxically, this happens even as we see how much of Him we don't yet understand. But trust in God stems from understanding His character, not His reasons. In relationship with Him we see daily His complete trustworthiness, goodness, power, and presence. We are never left alone or abandoned by Him. He never gives us reason to doubt Him (though sometimes we doubt out of our own propensity to question or do our own things).

Relationship with God is the best apologetic in the world. We will never argue anyone into salvation. A healthy, strong relationship with God is a beacon; it's inviting. People see it and want to know what it means and what it is. A strong relationship with God is the strength a Christian needs to stand up to withering scorn or rapier arguments. You may not be able to out-argue an opponent, but you will not be shaken in your belief. Because your belief is in the One you *know*, not in a concept.

THE PROCESS

Belief, even in relationship with God, is not black and white. We do not "arrive" at a place of satisfaction or finality. It is not like building a house where one day you stand back, dust off your hands, and think, *There. It's finished.* Belief is more like getting fit.

When you look around, it is clear that some people are fit and others are not. Many people, though, are sort of, maybe, a bit fit. But really you can't tell. They may be getting fit but don't quite look like it yet. They maybe used to be fit but got lazy or got jobs that interfered with their exercise routines. They're on the way down. No matter what, though, nobody gets fit by accident and nobody stays that way without effort.

Belief is like that. It does not just happen. It takes discipline and effort. Sometimes it is difficult, and sometimes we make massive progress. And sometimes we hit a wall. I have a friend who set out to lose weight. He began swimming and watching what he ate, and about five months later he had lost over forty pounds. Then the weight stopped coming off. He was still exercising just as rigorously and eating just as well, but he could not lose any more weight. So we changed his diet. He began lifting weights and running in addition to swimming. The new habits worked. A month and a half later he had lost another ten pounds. He had gotten stuck and then realized he needed to change both what he was ingesting and his routine. This is true for belief as well.

Maybe the next step for the fitness of your belief is a change in consumption—less of some things and more of others. Or find some new sustenance altogether. Health food enthusiasts are always expounding on the benefits of this super food or that natural supplement, and it changes almost seasonally, so much so that it's hard to keep up with. For belief, we have a true, unchanging super food: Scripture. God's Word is a revelation of Him, and to consume it is to fill yourself with what He wants you to know of Him.

Those of us who grew up in the church have been told all our lives —sometimes so often that it can become burdensome and like homework—to "read your Bible every day." That's why it's important to realize that we don't merely read our Bibles, we consume them. God's Word is sustenance to our souls, not merely suggestions or lessons or words of instruction. We *need* it to live. If we fill our souls with other things, it's similar to living on a diet of cotton candy. It might taste delicious at first, but after a while we get tired of it and feel ill. If it were all we ate, we would waste away because it has no nutritional value. Scripture is the nutrition our souls need, a regular multicourse dinner of it.

If you're like me, the phrase "read your Bible" almost triggers a gag reflex because of how often it has been thrown at you as a quick fix to a problem or commanded to you as the way to "get right with God." It wasn't until I recognized that reading my Bible was really hearing from God that it became rich and meaningful to me. In a relationship, we enjoy hearing from those we love and we are energized and helped by them, even if what they have to say is a hard word for us. We love to converse, exchange texts or emails, and spend time with loved ones. That is Scripture, God's correspondence and conversation with us. It is our way to spend time with Him. His Word is the sustenance we need, and remember, He gave us exactly what we need—no more and no less. (For more specifics on how to read the Bible this way, check out appendix 1, "Reading the Bible to Meet God.")

Maybe you already have a steady diet of biblical truth but have plateaued in belief. The change you need might be one of perspective, as I just mentioned. But maybe you simply need to change your routine to jump-start your spiritual metabolism. Instead of the same devotionals, podcasts, and study Bible find a new reading plan and some books by authors you've never read. Try music instead of podcasts (or vice versa).

Don't get caught up in the food-exercise-metabolism analogy, though. Scripture remains a living thing, the words of God to your soul. To change how you consume Scripture is not science, as in changing your eating habits. It's interactive. By doing something different, you are allowing new opportunities for the Holy Spirit to speak to you through Scripture. You are looking at Scripture from a different angle, from which you may see new and wonderful things about God. In the process your belief will become healthier and fitter.

But not perfectly healthy. Christians who live in the mindset of arriving, of reaching an end point, will inevitably become discouraged because they'll never get there. Remember, we live in the "not yet." Comparing belief to relationships or fitness can help us press on because both are perpetual areas for growth and cannot be left to themselves. But we must also consider God's infinity. As believers in Him how can we ever arrive? An understanding of Him cannot be contained in a human mind and heart. But that means we can always be growing. This is not an endless process of exhaustion and defeat; it's an eternal opportunity for growth in holiness! So we continue to pursue, to learn, to seek, to process. That is belief.

THE HOLY SPIRIT

Up to now I have hardly mentioned the Holy Spirit. That may be a mistake on my part. I waited so as not to confuse things by introducing too many ideas and variables all at once. I have written of various mysteries and unanswerable questions, and the Spirit points to yet another: the Trinity. Christians worship a God who is one and who is three in one. The Father, the Son, and the Holy Spirit are all God, but they are not separate gods. And they are not manifestations of God or separate "faces" of God; each of them is individual. Each one is distinct in His role and relationship with the other two. The Trinity is foundational to the Christian faith,[2] and while we are often comfortable speaking of God and Jesus, the Spirit is the silent, behind-the-scenes One so easy to forget. Without the Spirit, though, there would be no belief at all. So, late or not, I say this: the Holy Spirit is essential to *all* saving belief in Christ.

We cannot originate belief in ourselves. We cannot have relationship with God. We cannot understand truth. No transformation can happen. Not without the Holy Spirit.

The Holy Spirit is the introducer of our hearts to God. Our minds may have already absorbed countless facts about Him, but it is the Spirit who opens our hearts to Him. It is a miraculous introduction, the breaking through of the supernatural into our human hearts. And it is the Spirit who facilitates that new life.

> Holiness, as taught in the Scriptures, is not based upon knowledge on our part. Rather, it is based upon the resurrected Christ in-dwelling us and changing us into His likeness.[3]

> The moment the Spirit has quickened us to life in regeneration our whole being senses its kinship to God and leaps up in joyous recognition. That is the heavenly birth without which we cannot see the Kingdom of God.[4]
>
> —A. W. Tozer

While our minds, as creations of God, are capable of much understanding and knowledge, it is the Spirit who fires the synapses to grasp the connections from God's Word that lead us to true belief. People who have the Spirit in them will see life-transforming truth in a text where others will see only information. I wrote in chapter 3 about my friend Dr. Wayne Martindale telling me to read the Gospels and look for Jesus, and how seeing Jesus in those pages transformed my heart. But *why* could I see Jesus in a fresh way? I had read those same gospels dozens of times. I knew all the stories and sermons. What was different? Why did Scripture come alive? Because of the Spirit in me opening my heart to what my mind already knew. The Word of God is living and active, it is God breathed, and when the Spirit is acting in us, we become full of that life and breath.

The Spirit is also the One who gives the wisdom to know how to live what we have learned. The Bible calls the Spirit a "teacher" because He instructs our hearts to understand and to apply. The Spirit is called the "helper" because He indwells us (lives in us) and gives us the ability to do what our sin nature would otherwise reject and rebel against. All the good we do as Christians is powered by the Holy Spirit—the loving deeds, the kind words, the wise teaching, the rejection of temptation. He is the mover toward transformation.

In relationship with God we are inadequate to the task of prayer and often cannot express our hearts the way we want. But the Spirit takes our prayers before God and translates them into meaning. He is a go-between. He is also God's go-between to our hearts as He takes the words of Scripture and infuses them with life. Without the Spirit the Bible would be simply a lengthy book. With the Spirit it is "living and active, sharper than any two-edged sword."[5] It is a revelation of God's very self.

ONE MORE MYSTERY

So which came first, the Spirit or belief? The Spirit comes to us through belief in Jesus Christ, and yet the Spirit is also the One who opens our hearts to belief in Jesus Christ. How does it work? I cannot say.

I can simply say that I would not believe in Jesus if the Spirit had not softened my heart and shown me the profound grace of God. That was not an intellectual decision. My decision to follow Jesus is one that I cannot help but make because I have seen the promise of the gospel, and it was the Spirit who showed me. He shows me daily, so I continue to believe.

> The wind blows wherever it pleases. You hear its sound, but you cannot tell where it comes from or where it is going. So it is with everyone born of the Spirit.[6]
>
> —Apostle John

Nobody can systematize or categorize the movements of the Spirit. He moves where He will and stirs the most frozen hearts. He brings about belief in the least likely hearts. He raises the deadest souls to life. And He found me when I was on the verge of walking away from Jesus: For the first time I saw the wonder of grace and my need for it. I didn't make that happen. The Spirit came and got me.

Why? I do not know. How? Because the Spirit is part of the Godhead. I don't understand, and I don't think anyone is supposed to. I do know that He moved in power. This is how belief happens. Sometimes the Spirit comes in gently and nudges a heart toward God. Other times He grabs the steering wheel of the heart and jerks it into the path of God's oncoming grace. A beautiful collision it is when a soul driving toward a cliff called rebellion and self-rule is steered back into the path of God's grace. In a magnificently violent moment the old self is killed, and in its place is put a self filled with God's Spirit, filled with hope, filled with peace, and pointed down the road toward the "not yet." The new self will struggle to drive straight. It will drift and even turn hard toward that cliff, but God did not leave it alone. He left it a helper who will guide, teach, and steer it in the way it should go.

Alone we are blind. The Spirit gives sight. Alone we are foolish. The Spirit gives wisdom. Alone we are dead. The Spirit gives life.

Chapter 8

SO WHAT AND
WHAT NOW?

What was the point of all this? Did we actually arrive anywhere or gain any sense of where to go moving forward? Most books try to "land the plane" at some point, to give a destination. Will I do the same for you? Yes! And no, not really.

YES, THIS IS WHERE YOU GO

Here's where we land—you have an aim. You have a direction in which to move. When you set this book down after a few more pages of reading, I trust you will sense it. While I have not given you all the answers for every question and I have not settled your mind or heart, I hope to have pointed the way.

Process of Belief

Your course is one of process. You will never "arrive at belief"; you live in the "not yet." But because it is not *yet*, you have the assurance it is coming—perfect belief will come. And you must go to it.

This process, this "not yet," is a comfort. It provides an assurance of peace to come. It is a promise made by the omnipotent, sovereign God so as you go you can live in the surety of belief coming. Perfect peace of mind and fullness of heart will one day be yours if you continue in the pursuit of belief now, no matter how distant they seem in this torturous life.

The process is a motivation as well. God does not promise resolution to those who refuse the process. If you are unwilling to think, to change, to work, to grow, there is no promise for you because you have rebelled against the perfect God. God's promise is fulfilled *through* the process of belief in Jesus. So we have the motivation we need to get where God has promised to take us. Our lives are based on a promise of "not yet" fulfilled through Jesus's life for those who continue on in belief.

A Right Understanding of God

In the "not yet" we cannot arrive at perfect belief, but we can gain a right understanding of God. This doesn't mean a complete knowledge of Him; as we've seen, that's impossible. It means a right awareness of, and belief in, His nature in relation to ours. All the problems in the world, every single one of them, stem from getting this backward. Adam and Eve thought they could know what God knows, they thought they knew what was best for themselves, and they put themselves on par with God. Ever since then things have been fouled up.

"I am who I am": five words in Exodus 3:14 that sum up who God is and who we are not. "I am" is a statement of His being and His character. It is a declaration of His eternity, His infinity in time, space, knowledge, and perfection. He is immutable and everlasting. For all of time, even before time was time, He was. And He will be so after time ceases to be.

And they are five words nobody else can say, not like He can. I am any number of adjectives but none of the ones that I just used to describe God. You are lots of different things too and have many traits. You are unique and amazingly created. But you are not *I AM*. Because you are *created*. God is I AM because He always has been.

We must daily put ourselves in a position to see this, to recognize it, to abide by it. We do this by going back continually to God's revelation of Himself, because in those pages we see Him as He wants to be seen, in power and grace. We do this by opening our eyes to the world around us. Look at the created universe, the music, the cultures, the colors, the tiniest insects, the most mammoth beasts, the mountains, the surf, the breezes, the flowers, and the trees. Then recognize that this incomprehensible array of magnificence sits on a terrestrial ball in the middle of a galaxy that makes up a speck in the universe over which God rules. The I AM created all this and rules it yesterday, today, and forever. The foundation of belief, to become what we are supposed to become, is to live with the belief that He is I AM and we are not. To resist this ties us to the garden of Eden and shows the sinful nature we inherited from that forlorn couple who ate the fruit.

Childlike Faith

"Truly, I say to you, unless you turn and become like children, you will never enter the kingdom of heaven."[1] What does it mean to become "like children"? You have likely heard that Christians should have "faith like a child." Either way, though, the imagery is opaque. Children don't come in one size, shape, or temperament.

Even a single family will have children who are feisty, passive, tall, short, organized, and free spirited (and that only applies to my two daughters). When we think on what we've seen of belief, we can understand some of what Jesus meant when He commanded us to be like little children.

He didn't tell us to be "like a babe-in-arms." Childlike faith is not passive, mindless dependence. A little child is active, incredibly so. She is curious about everything. She explores and questions and wants to know. But as we saw earlier, children do not ask out of skepticism. Little children ask because they want to learn and because they expect their parents to have answers. Of course, as any parent knows, sometimes the answer is "Because it's what's best" or "Because I'm Dad and I said so." Little children might huff and puff and stomp a bit, but in the end, these answers work for them. They believe that Dad or Mom has their best interest in mind, and they don't get hung up in some sort of existential limbo over why; they just trust.

And then they obey. Not perfectly. Not always. But a child who has been raised by attentive parents generally does what she ought. Because Dad or Mom taught her well and because she has seen, intuitively, that peace and happiness reside in obedience.

A problem arises because we grow out of childhood. We begin to seek independence. We question because we begin to think we know more than our parents. And we decisively rebel against them. In time we find out that our parents are imperfect and don't, in fact, know everything. Sometimes what they think is best isn't. Sometimes obeying doesn't mean peace and happiness; sometimes it leads to hurt and frustration. And we act the same way toward God that we do toward them.

God, however, doesn't ever make mistakes. We don't ever out-grow our need of Him. We don't outlearn Him. And we never find that He made a decision that hurt us or had ill motives. Good par-ents love their children deeply and always try to do what's best, but God is a *perfect* Father. His love is endless. His motives are flawless. When He says, "Because I'm Dad and I said so," we have no room to doubt whether He is right.

So, like a little child (not a baby, not an adolescent), we ask and we question and we act all in a context of "Dad knows best." Children do not expect to understand everything their parents know, and they wouldn't want to if given the opportunity. It would be too much for their little minds—too stressful, too tedious, too confus-ing. So it is with us and God. His "knowledge is too wonderful for me, too lofty for me to attain."[2]

We have "matured" beyond faith. We think if we don't know the answer it can't exist. How arrogant! Children would never think that. They would believe, possibly misguidedly, that their fathers know the answers. But our Father *always* knows, regardless of our capacity to understand. So we ask, we act, we explore, and we obey. Because Dad knows best, and He proves His love over and over again.

Connected to Jesus

In the wonderful book *Walking with God through Pain and Suffering*, Tim Keller answered many of the deepest questions pertaining to faith. In one portion Keller drew on the book of Job and quoted, at points, sociologist Peter Berger.

In the Old Testament book of Job, we have the most difficult and severe truth about suffering—namely, that in the end we cannot question God. Job calls on God to explain why such sorrows and griefs have come upon him. But in response "the questioner is radically challenged to his right to pose questions in the first place." God confronts Job with his own finitude, his inability to understand God's counsels and purposes even if they were revealed, and his status as a sinner in no position to demand a comfortable life. Berger admits that this view of things has a strong logic to it, but that all by itself such a vision would be "hard to sustain for most people."[3]

At this point, I wonder if maybe I have left some readers with the impression that God is unapproachable. Maybe I have presented a view of God that is huge and powerful and, in one important sense, unquestionable (all three are true). But I agree with Berger when he said such a view of God is "hard to sustain," at least in any sense other than cognitive. I resonate with that distance if that is all God is. Several years ago I was having a conversation with a group of friends and one of them, a young mom, was expressing her frustration with this view of God. She said to some of us, "Your view of God is big and powerful and distant. What about the God who cares when my kids are eating peanut butter sandwiches or skin their knees? I want a God who loves me and cares about the little things!" I've never looked at PB&J sandwiches quite the same way since.

God is big and powerful and beyond us. But He is anything but distant! In fact, He is the exact opposite through His incarnate Son. Keller went on to say:

> The answer of the book of Job—that "God knows what he's doing, so be quiet and trust him"—is right but insufficient. It is inadequate because alone it is cold and because the New Testament gives us more with which to face the terrors of life. We turned from God, but God did not abandon us.... God came to earth in Jesus Christ and became subject to suffering and death himself.[4]

Keller's thoughts are an expansion of what we see in Romans 5:8: "God shows his love for us in that while we were still sinners, Christ died for us." This is the God of Job, the God of creation, the all-powerful God who is too great to be understood. And He *loves* us. Jesus is the living, dying, resurrected, reigning proof of that.

Jesus is our personal connection to God. He "always lives to intercede"[5] for us. That means Jesus is our advocate to God, the God who is too holy and perfect for us to come to on our own. But this isn't Jesus versus God. It was God who sent Jesus to be our advocate. That was the "already"; Jesus came and died and rose again. Now Jesus continues to work on our behalf in the "not yet." And all of this is the will of the I AM who is too great for us to understand.

Jesus is the mercy of God.[6]

—Art Azurdia

So we pursue a relationship with Jesus. In the "not yet" we live for Him and we live through Him. We come to Him from different places and connect in different ways. But it is the same Jesus who provides the way to God, the promise of hope and life and perfect peace. It is Jesus in whom we believe and who helps our unbelief. He is where we look, for whom we live, and whom we trust.

NO, WE'RE NOT THERE YET

We have an aim and a trajectory. But we still live in this temporal life, the life of "not yet," and for that reason I cannot leave you with neat and tidy instructions to make you feel good. Belief doesn't work that way. (In fact, little in this life works that way despite what all the self-improvement and business books and blogs would lead you to believe.) We are always becoming—becoming something better or something worse. We never arrive this side of heaven.

An Ongoing Process

Just as a process of belief is our trajectory, it is also the main reason I cannot tie up all the loose ends of this book. There are no quick fixes to a sinful nature or a finite mind. There is no encyclopedia of answers to the mysteries of God. There is no resting on our laurels for growth in Christlikeness or strengthening of faith.

Sometimes when I finish a book I feel as though I've just earned several sanctification points. It's as if I just ate a spinach and kale salad and can feel good about how healthy I am now. But books don't work that way. They are only as valuable as the actions they inspire us to take and the mind-sets they help transform. I don't want you to set this book down and feel good about yourself. You get no sanctification points from this.

For some, I hope this book offers peace and your life can become easier because you can now see that the tensions you feel in your faith are not bad things. I hope it points you to a future of rest and lets you know that not knowing is okay. Do your searching. Ask your questions. Then find peace in the knowledge of a good and sovereign God to whom we can go through a present and personal Jesus.

For others, I hope this book unsettles you. Too long have you rested in "the Bible says it, I believe it, that settles it." I don't think it's all that settled. More likely you have been afraid of questions—afraid they would offend your fellow Christians or even offend God, afraid they would rattle your faith. What if those questions are not, in fact, settled? What then? Do you have an answer, or are you too frightened to look for one? And even worse, what if you're unable to find one? For you, I hope this book moves you to boldness in your questions and venturing outside the fabricated safety of an untested faith. Go forth and face the wild things, take your lumps, and know that God will not leave you or forsake you as you do.

Everyone must take action. Christians must take action. Belief, real belief, is seen in action. For some, that means learning to follow Jesus without the frenetic, fearful, skeptical searching. For others, it means getting up, taking steps, and realizing faith is not a simple thing. It means a little exploring would expand your relationship with Jesus enormously. Either way, be in process. Do not sit idly, feeling as if reading this book (or any other) is an accomplishment all its own.

No Two Circumstances Are Alike

Part of our progression of belief is recognizing the uniqueness of each person's individual growth. Too often in Christianity we create neat grids, systematized structures, step-by-step processes, or simplistic narratives to explain how belief comes about and what it looks like. We can't do that. While we know the ingredients of real belief, we do not understand—not *really* understand—its origin. We know where it comes from (the Holy Spirit working in a person) but not *how* it happens. Life-transforming belief is a miracle. It happens outside of human reason and scientific explanation.

No two people have the same experience of belief. We don't share our unique testimonies or struggles or doubts or fears with anyone else. We can't project our experiences onto others and assume we know what they're going through. How I connect with God—the circumstances or lessons He used to bring me to Himself—will differ from how you connect with Him. Belief is an intensely personal thing, a process and experience I hold in my heart that nobody else holds.

And yet God raised up the church, a body of believers to show the world what it means to believe and follow. Millions of people with disparate stories and experiences are tasked with coming together to exemplify and preach belief to the world. In God's infinite wisdom the best way to bring more people to belief is to show them a massively varied story pointed in one direction—to Himself. Nobody's faith story is the same as anyone else's, but the collective experience of the church crosses borders of culture, emotion, brokenness, pain, doubt, or fear. What we share, the object of our belief, is the thread woven through all the narratives.

> A community, a family, is a group of people who share common stories. The health of any community depends directly on the health of the stories the community embraces.[7]
>
> —Daniel Taylor

As believers, we must work continually toward this collective narrative. The church is a body, conjoined parts creating a whole that is greater than the sum of the parts. My story, though different from yours, complements yours. Each of our individual stories is born out of belief in a single story—that of God's redemption of the world. As more believers are woven into the impact of the story, belief grows exponentially. Even though I do not have the same story as someone else, I recognize God in both our stories, I see new ways of God working that I did not yet know, and I discover answers to questions I did not yet even know to ask. And this happens time and again, millions of times over as believers connect in the church.

But this takes effort. It does not just happen. While belief joins us together, sin drives us apart. While God's work now defines us, sin still marks us. We live in the "not yet." But we live here *with* fellow believers. We bring our unique experiences of belief to the table and share them with others doing the same. Some of what they bring strengthens us and encourages us. But some of it may hurt us. Spend just a little time in a church community and you will encounter the same friction you find in families and office spaces: gossiping, conflicting personalities, selfishness. You will learn that your sins cause damage and other people's sins damage you. On this side of the "not yet" we cannot escape the effects of sin. That is why it is essential to remember the work of Christ.

> Whoever believes in him shall not perish but have eternal life.[8]

> I have not come to call the righteous but sinners to repentance.[9]

> I am the way and the truth and the life.[10]

> The gift of God is eternal life in Christ Jesus our Lord.[11]

> If anyone is in Christ, he is a new creation.[12]

Jesus overcomes the difficulties and hurts of communing with other sinners. He bridges the gaps, heals the wounds, and lifts the fallen. He fills our hearts with love and empathy for those we see nothing in common with, who frighten us, who annoy us. We must point to Jesus, remember Jesus, hold to Jesus. Our belief, though our own, can then show Jesus to others. How do others see Jesus in us even though they live in their own circumstances and struggles? I do not know, but God does. It is how He ordained to bring people into belief, into eternal life, into the joy of the promise of the "not yet."

"I Don't Know" Is Okay

Nobody likes loose ends (except the occasional film student who thrives on avant-garde movies that end in the middle and resolve nothing). We thrive on happy endings and solving the puzzles. Sherlock Holmes is read, reread, and turned into endless spin-off TV and movie franchises because he ties up all the loose ends in such pithy fashion. Politicians and media members will hem and haw and spin and redirect rather than admit they do not know the answer to a question. To make things more personal, we hate not knowing why tragedy happens. We hate not being able to explain science and history. "I don't know" is the most unsatisfactory phrase we know.

It's also one of the most human. We simply cannot know many things, not because we aren't allowed, but because we aren't capable. In the garden of Eden, Adam and Eve tried to gain knowledge that was beyond them, and through them the rest of us have been cursed with the same compulsion ever since. We want to know what only God can know. But we are created beings, created by God. We are created within time and space and scientific laws. We have physical, mental, and emotional limitations. It is not that we have yet to learn or understand certain pieces of knowledge. It's that we will never be able to. Like it or not, such is the nature of being human.

We will live with loose ends, and that is something we must accept, not because they are inherently good, but because there is an inherently good God. We live in faith, and faith, by nature, stems from an "I don't know." Hebrews tells us that "faith is the assurance of things hoped for, the conviction of things not seen."[13] We hope; we don't see. To live by faith is to rest in the object of our faith, the God of the Bible, and to come to terms with all of our "I don't knows."

We pursue knowledge about God, about life, about the world. But we must recognize when "I don't know" becomes "I can't know," when we've reached the limits of our human minds and hearts. That is where the prayer "Help my unbelief" matters most because the temptation is to doubt, to question God's character, to drift toward self-deifying and self-gratifying demands. For some, the limits are found through intellectual angst, perpetual questioning. They always proceed to the next question until there are no more answers. What then? Then "Help my unbelief." For many, though, the limits are reached because the experiences of life overwhelm what their minds know. A close friend or family member dies. A spouse cheats on them. An employer fires them. A child estranges them. And they run out of capacity to explain or understand how and why God is doing things. What then? Then "Help my unbelief." At the limits of our knowledge and understanding is where belief is the most important and the most difficult. So we say to the God we are wrestling with, "I believe; help my unbelief."

> To one who has faith, no explanation is necessary. To one without faith, no explanation is possible.[14]
>
> —Thomas Aquinas

Faith is a reasoning trust, a trust which reckons thoughtfully and confidently upon the trustworthiness of God.[15]

—John Stott

HOPE

My hope for you, reader, is that this book will point you toward peace. Maybe I have stirred up more questions than I have answered, but I believe those questions are important ones to work through for the health of your faith. You may have a hard row to hoe before you find peace.

For others, I hope this book pointed you to a mind-set that settles some of your questions, even if it doesn't answer them. You may need to lay your questions down and recognize they can't be answered, not while you're in the "not yet." But you can still find rest in the character of God and the work of Jesus. They are richer, deeper, fuller, and more wonderful than any answer you hoped to find. In fact, in the character of God and the work of Jesus are the answers you needed even if they aren't what you expected.

HELP

"I believe; help my unbelief" represents the tension, the need, the promise for every follower of Jesus. We do believe. We do live every day in great need. Our belief is imperfect, so we cry out for help. But that cry comes from a place of belief. We hold fast to God even as we feel pulled by the current of doubt, fear, and temptation.

Pray this daily. Let it remind you of what you know of God and what you don't yet know, what you rest in and what you look forward to. Pray it so that your faith is strengthened and your sin is overcome. Pray it so that you never fall into the trap of thinking you have arrived and so that you can live well in the process of belief. Pray it so that you can live a believing life in the "not yet" while looking forward to glory.

AFTERWORD

No book outside the Word of God is the final word on anything. Every one is a contribution to dialogue, to a narrative, to a process. I did not write this book thinking it would "seal the deal" for most readers' beliefs. I wrote it in the hopes it would move them forward in belief.

I am distinctly aware of my own inadequacy to convince anyone to believe anything and of the holes in this book. It's as I wrote in chapter 7 about the church: each individual story matters but none is the same as another. This book contains bits of my story. That will connect with some readers and won't with others. I tried to offset story with argumentation and scriptural backing to tie it all together.

In the end, what I hope readers take from these pages is a clearer vision of God and the wonderful reality of relationship with Him. There really is hope nowhere else; so no matter what unbelief tells you, don't give up on it. This "not yet" you live in can be brutal, miserable at times, but it will end. If you hang on to your relationship with God, you will find happiness beyond explanation on the other side.

Appendix 1

READING THE BIBLE
TO MEET GOD

In chapter 7, I wrote about how important it is to read the Bible to meet God, to read it relationally and as sustenance for the soul. That sounds like a great idea and the ideal for a Christian, but how do we actually do it? How can we change our mind-sets to view Scripture as a living, rich revelation instead of a religious tome of instructions and history? Here are seven ways.

1. READ THE WHOLE STORY.

Many of us learned to read God's Word from children's Bible storybooks made up of individual stories—Adam and Eve, David and Goliath, Jonah and the big fish (of course it was Jonah and the *whale* back then), the boy's five loaves and two fish, and so on. We learned to look for stories, snippets of Scripture. And usually these came with a moral lesson about trusting God, making the right decisions, being honest, serving others, or something else.

The other main way we heard the Bible taught was character centric, like a series of mini-bios. We studied the lives of Abraham, Joseph, Ruth, Saul, Solomon, Esther, Peter, and Paul. We were taught about their shortcomings and their faithfulness. We learned that they were examples for us to follow, just not perfect ones.

While we gleaned a lot of truth from these lessons, the teaching method actually misguided us. We learned to read the Scripture similar to how we skim through a magazine: a story here, skip the boring bits, a profile there, and some good info throughout if you know where to look. But the Bible is not like that at all. It is a narrative made up of different parts. It must be read in full.

We must learn to read the whole story of Scripture from beginning to end. The Bible is God's story of redemption, the revelation of Himself and His plan for the world. All those stories and all those characters are parts of the whole, characters in the drama, but none of them are *the* point. They all point to the point: Jesus Christ came, lived a perfect life, died an innocent death to save sinners and kill death and sin, and will one day return to right all the wrongs. Sure, some parts of the Bible are confusing and dry, but they fit in the whole too. And when we understand that there is a whole narrative, even those parts start to make sense in their context.

Reading the Bible this way may seem like a tall task, especially if you haven't been in the habit of reading it much at all. If so, start small, bit by bit. Take notes. Ask questions. In the next appendix, I recommend several books, some of which can help explain how it all fits together. Piece by piece, little by little, you'll begin to see the big story of the Bible, and it will become so much greater than you thought possible in Sunday school.

2. LOOK FOR JESUS.

It was the advice that helped change my perspective on Scripture and the advice I would suggest to any Christian who finds the Bible to be stale and lifeless: look for Jesus. So much of what we miss in Scripture is because we look for characters and themes and lessons other than Jesus. But He is both the primary character and the primary plotline of Scripture. To look for anything else first is to rip out the heart of God's Word. Because Jesus, as John 1 tells us, *is* the Word made flesh.

Every page of Scripture points to Jesus. It all fits together to point to Him and to glorify Him and depict Him and reveal Him. In the first point I said to read the whole story. Well, that's because the whole story is the story of the need for Jesus, the promise of Jesus, the life of Jesus, the work of Jesus, the death and resurrection of Jesus, and ultimately the victory of Jesus.

When we read the whole story and see Jesus throughout the pages, we see Him afresh, not as whatever preconceived notions we had. We see Him as more than a teacher, more than a healer, more than a model character. We see the breadth of Jesus from the man who sat with children and loved widows to the sword-wielding King of justice and glory.

3. WHEN YOU SEE JESUS, GET TO KNOW HIM.

Observations about Jesus are the stuff of sermons and Sunday school lessons and Christian books like this one. But in the Bible we have the means to get to *know* Jesus. We have the means to move past observation and awareness and fact-finding to a real, personal connection with Him. How? Like we do in any relationship.

Make it a regular thing. Go back to those Gospels over and over again. God's Word is inexhaustible and can always deepen your understanding and belief. We don't limit ourselves in conversation with our loved ones because we "talked to them already," and neither should we limit ourselves in the reading of the Bible because we "read it already." It is as dynamic and deep, in fact even deeper, than any person we seek to know.

Ask questions of Jesus in Scripture. Ask about His character. Ask about His values. Ask about His life. Ask about His priorities. Ask about His weaknesses. And let Scripture respond to you. The answers you find will lead you to want to know more, to be closer, to be *with* Jesus. And the more we are with Him, the more we will find ourselves learning to be and wanting to be like Him.

4. DON'T SHY AWAY FROM THE HARD STUFF.

One of the most significant weaknesses of most Bible teaching in the traditional church is the void where all the hard stuff in the Bible happens. Not until I got to college did I ever hear mention of the rape of Dinah or God commanding the destruction of entire people groups. Nobody talked about the flood except as a means to a rainbow. Nobody answered questions about where Cain found his wife if his parents were the first people ever. Nobody explained what it meant for an omnipotent, omniscient God to relent and change His mind or how He could harden Pharaoh's heart, then judge him for rebellion. What in the world are we supposed to do with that stuff?

Well, I can tell you what we're not supposed to do: ignore it. Pretending it doesn't exist doesn't delete it from the Bible. If God hadn't wanted us to see it, know it, and think on it, He wouldn't have filled up His self-revelation with it.

We must read it and consider it. We must be willing to wrestle with it. We have to look at it, not as a bunch of isolated incidents and texts that might be problematic, but as part of the whole. If we are going to read the whole story and look for how it all points to Jesus, then we need to see how the hard stuff fits in. It likely isn't a straight-line connection, but each difficult passage connects to something else that connects to something that points to Jesus. It is all there on purpose, and it all paints a picture of God.

Just because we don't understand doesn't mean we can reject it. As we've seen throughout this book, thinking that way is to determine who God is, based on our own intellectual abilities. We don't get to do that. We must see what Scripture says, look at it in context, see it as part of the whole, and recognize that it is all part of a portrait of God that expands far beyond our minds and hearts.

5. START SMALL, PERHAPS WITH CHILDREN'S BOOKS, AND MIX IN OTHER RESOURCES TOO.

Sola Scriptura: by Scripture alone—one of the foundational doctrines of Protestant Christianity. It means that our only holy book is the Bible, our only word of God is the Bible, our only doctrine is found in the Bible. The Bible is the foundation on which our faith is built. But it does not mean we read only the Bible. In fact, other books by godly writers can serve to open up our minds and hearts to Scripture.

HELP MY UNBELIEF • 160

Some of the best materials are those written for children. (I know, I know; I pointed out the weaknesses in children's Bibles earlier.) In appendix 2, I recommend two children's Bible storybooks in particular, *The Big Picture Story Bible* and *The Jesus Storybook Bible*. After graduating from college and gaining a theology degree, after working in Christian publishing for several years and reading mountains of biblical teaching books, I still find these the freshest, best entry points into the message of the Bible. They make it fun by bringing out the story, and they make their points with clarity and gentleness. I am sure other similar resources are out there as well. They make an ideal starting point to begin enjoying Scripture and piecing together its message.

Additional resources and books will be helpful too. Some will prefer a commentary; others will gravitate to a Bible study curriculum. Each serves a great purpose in helping us dig in and understand more. Don't shy away from them. Find the ones that fit your learning style, and take full advantage of them. The thing to always remember is to not let the study of the Bible become the end. Knowledge of Scripture can be an idol all by itself, but it must always be a means to closeness to God.

6. DON'T READ THE BIBLE AS A SET OF RULES BUT RATHER AS A BOOK.

So many Christians lose touch with the heart of Scripture because for so long they have approached it under the rule of law. "You must read your Bible every day." Reading your Bible every day is a great thing, but within its very pages it describes how the law introduces us to sin. When we make rules out of things, we tend to take the life out of them, no matter how good they are.

We need to approach the Bible as a book. After all, that is the form in which God gave it to us. For those who love to read, this means conscientiously moving it to the category of great literature in our minds, a great story, deep philosophy, a rich biography. When we think of it that way, we will see different things in its pages, yes, but more importantly we will be able to overcome the greatest mental block to reading it at all.

For those who do not enjoy reading, I wonder how you made it all the way to this point in a book! More seriously, though, think of the Bible the same way, but find a different format in which to consume it. Reading is not for everyone, but the Bible is. So find a way to eat up this wonderful story, teaching, and biography. Audio Bibles are great tools. They may be the perfect answer for you, or they may be the gateway you need to get into the written text. Either way, avail yourself of them!

Regardless of how you do it, though, no matter the medium, distance yourself from the legalistic guilt of reading the Bible as law. That robs it of its wonder and steals the joy from your heart. It is so rich and deep; read it to discover and wonder!

7. PRAY FOR THE SPIRIT'S HELP.

We have a helper and a teacher. Jesus even said we would be better off if He left because this helper is so amazing. Really? We're better off without Jesus on earth with us? Yes! Because the Holy Spirit dwells in every Christian, moving us toward being more like Jesus, teaching our minds, and softening and convicting our hearts.

Only by the Spirit will *anything* I just wrote about reading the Bible matter at all. If you seek to do any of this in your own power, you will dry up, run out of motivation, get bored, become arrogant, lose faith, get confused, and turn from God. It is inevitable. The Bible is not a normal book. It is a book spoken out by God to be interpreted to our hearts by God the Spirit. It is a supernatural book.

To connect with God through His Word is a miracle of the Spirit and not something that can be formulated. All the suggestions I just made are not the equation that adds up to relationship with God. They are ingredients that must be present, but only the Spirit can mix and prepare them in such a way that we see God in His glory and are moved to follow and honor Him. So beg the Spirit to open your eyes when you read. Plead with the Spirit to give you the inspiration to read. And He will. Maybe not in a flash, but He will. And as you delve deeper into God's Word, you will find that the Spirit and God's message in the Bible will change you.

Appendix 2

SUGGESTED READING

The books in this list are ones that, at various times, have shaped and directed my faith. Each of them depicts something of what it means to believe or to struggle with belief. Some are stories. Some are arguments. Some are reflections. I encourage you to find the one or ones with which you connect and consume them with delight.

The Skeptical Believer by Daniel Taylor
The Myth of Certainty by Daniel Taylor
The Man Called Cash by Steve Turner
The Reason for God by Tim Keller
Surprised by Joy by C. S. Lewis
The Big Story by Justin Buzzard
The End of Our Exploring by Matthew Lee Anderson
Death by Living by N. D. Wilson
Notes from the Tilt-a-Whirl by N. D. Wilson
Mere Christianity by C. S. Lewis
God in the Dock by C. S. Lewis
Orthodoxy by G. K. Chesterton
Simply Christian by N. T. Wright
Knowing God by J. I. Packer
Counterfeit Gods by Tim Keller
The Jesus Storybook Bible by Sally Lloyd-Jones

The Big Picture Story Bible by David Helm

God's Big Picture by Vaughan Roberts

Searching for God Knows What by Donald Miller

NOTES

INTRODUCTION

1. Barnabas Piper, *The Pastor's Kid: Finding Your Own Faith and Identity* (Colorado Springs, CO: David C Cook, 2014).
2. John 3:16.
3. Revelation 21:4.

CHAPTER 1: TENSION

1. Mark 9:20–27.
2. In the famous 1973 film *The Exorcist*, Linda Blair's character, Regan, is possessed by a demon. During one iconic scene she vomits out a disgusting substance. In reality the discharge was made of pea soup and oatmeal.
3. Robert Farrar Capon, *Hunting the Divine Fox*, in *The Romance of the Word: One Man's Love Affair with Theology* (Grand Rapids, MI: Eerdmans, 1995), 250.
4. Immanuel Kant, *Critique of Pure Reason*, trans. Max Mueller (New York: Doubleday, 1966), xxxix.
5. Richard Dawkins, *The God Delusion* (Boston: Mariner, 2008), 77.
6. For a helpful and accessible exploration of asking well, read Matthew Lee Anderson's *The End of Our Exploring: A Book about Questioning and the Confidence of Faith* (Chicago: Moody, 2013).

7. Elisabeth Elliot, *Passion and Purity: Learning to Bring Your Love Life under Christ's Control* (Grand Rapids, MI: Revell, 2006), 61–62.

8. Luke 22:42 NIV.

9. Mark 15:34 NIV.

10. Matthew 19:16–22.

CHAPTER 2: WHAT IS BELIEF?

1. The five *solas* are the defining doctrines of Protestant Christianity as developed in the Reformation, the church's revival during the 1400s and 1500s. They are Latin phrases explaining key doctrines: *sola fide* (by faith alone), *sola gratia* (by grace alone), *solus Christus* (through Christ alone), *sola Scriptura* (in Scripture alone), and *soli Deo gloria* (to God alone be the glory). They were created specifically to address Roman Catholic practices and theology, such as reward and merit, the sacrament of holy orders (unique rights and privileges of the clergy), and apostolic succession, including the infallibility and position of the pope.

2. For a helpful look at demonic activity and how Christians should interact with it, read Mark Bubeck's *The Adversary: The Christian versus Demon Activity* (Chicago: Moody, 2013).

3. Thomas Fuller, quoted in Bob Kelly, ed., *Worth Repeating: More Than 5,000 Classic and Contemporary Quotes* (Grand Rapids, MI: Kregel, 2003), 27.

4. Joni Eareckson Tada, *Joni and Friends* radio broadcast, Joni and Friends ministry, date unknown.

CHAPTER 3: WHAT CAN WE KNOW ABOUT GOD?

1. Harry Emerson Fosdick, "The Mystery of Life," in *Riverside Sermons* (New York: Harper, 1958), 22.

2. Tracy M. Sumner, ed., "Faith," in *The Essential Works of Andrew Murray: 12 Complete Books Covering the Entire Christian Life* (Uhrichsville, OH: Barbour, 2008), ebook.

3. "Oswald Chambers: Quotes," Goodreads, accessed December 26, 2014, www.goodreads.com/author/quotes/41469.Oswald _Chambers.

4. "Quote by Richard Dawkins," Richard Dawkins Foundation for Science and Reason, accessed December 26, 2014, http://old. richarddawkins.net/quotes/20.

5. Deism is a belief system dating back to the seventeenth century that states there is a supreme deity who created the world and should be worshipped but who does not interfere in the doings of the world. Deism developed primarily out of the dissatisfaction people felt with organized religion and the failures of the church.

6. Isaiah 45:7.

7. For a fantastic explanation of worldviews, God, and suffering, read Tim Keller's *Walking with God through Pain and Suffering* (New York: Dutton, 2013). The book offers a more philosophically detailed explanation of different views and how each fails to represent rightly God and a good answer for suffering.

8. Job 38:1–12.

9. Job 40:4 NIV.

10. Thomas Watson, *A Body of Divinity* (n.p.: Indo-European Publishing, 2014), 95.

11. Psalm 136:1–9.

CHAPTER 4: A PRAYER FROM WHERE?

1. Frederick Buechner, *The Magnificent Defeat* (New York: HarperCollins, 1985), 35.

CHAPTER 5: UNBELIEF AND DOUBT

1. Friedrich Nietzsche, *Daybreak: Thoughts on the Prejudices of Morality*, ed. Maudemarie Clark and Brian Leiter (Cambridge: Cambridge University Press, 2003), 52.

2. Paul Tillich, *Systematic Theology*, vol. 2 (Chicago: University of Chicago Press, 1975), 116.

3. Søren Kierkegaard, paraphrased in Donald D. Palmer, *Kierkegaard for Beginners* (Danbury, CT: For Beginners Books, 1996), 54.

4. Matthew 23:27.

5. Dietrich Bonhoeffer, *The Cost of Discipleship* (New York: Touchstone, 1995), 285.

CHAPTER 6: BELIEF IN ACTION

1. Søren Kierkegaard, quoted in *The Westminster Collection of Christian Quotations: Over 6,000 Quotations Arranged by Theme*, comp. Martin H. Manser (Louisville: Westminster John Knox, 2001), 261.

2. Martin Luther King Jr., paraphrased in "MLK Quote of the Week," The King Center, February 21, 2013, www.thekingcenter.org /blog/mlk-quote-week-faith-taking-first-step.

3. C. S. Lewis, *Mere Christianity* (New York: HarperOne, 2001), 147–48.

4. Genesis 15:6 NIV.

5. Genesis 22:8 NIV.

6. Genesis 22:12 NIV.

7. *Works of Ralph Waldo Emerson* (London: Routledge, 1897), 502.

8. Madeleine L'Engle, *A Wind in the Door* (New York: Square Fish, 2007), 153.

9. Revelation 21:3–5 NIV.

10. Lewis, *Mere Christianity*, 137.

CHAPTER 7: HOW DO WE BELIEVE?

1. 1 Corinthians 3:6.

2. For a fantastic explanation of God as the Trinity and why it is so important to the Christian faith, read Fred Sanders's *The Deep Things of God: How the Trinity Changes Everything* (Wheaton, IL: Crossway, 2010).

3. James L. Snyder, comp. and ed., "The Blessed Hope and the Curse of Curiosity" in *A. W. Tozer: Preparing for Jesus' Return: Daily Live the Blessed Hope* (Bloomington, MN: Bethany, 2012), ebook.

4. A. W. Tozer, *The Pursuit of God* (Rockville, MD: Serenity, 2009), 16.

5. Hebrews 4:12.

6. John 3:8 NIV.

CHAPTER 8: SO WHAT AND WHAT NOW?

1. Matthew 18:3.

2. Psalm 139:6 NIV.

3. Timothy Keller, *Walking with God through Pain and Suffering* (New York: Dutton, 2014), 114. The Peter L. Berger quotes are from *The Sacred Canopy: Elements of a Sociological Theory of Religion* (New York: Anchor, 1967), 74–75.

4. Keller, *Walking*, 121.

5. Hebrews 7:25 NIV.

6. From a sermon preached by Art Azurdia as heard on Beautiful Eulogy's "Blessed Are the Merciful," *Instruments of Mercy* © 2013 Humble Beast.

7. Daniel Taylor, "In Praise of Stories," in *The Christian Imagination: The Practice of Faith in Literature and Writing*, rev. ed., ed. Leland Ryken (Colorado Springs: WaterBrook, 2008), 410.

8. John 3:16 NIV.

9. Luke 5:32.

10. John 14:6 NIV.

11. Romans 6:23 NIV.

12. Second Corinthians 5:17.

13. Hebrews 11:1.

14. Thomas Aquinas, quoted in *The Ultimate Book of Quotations*, comp. Joseph Demakis (Raleigh: Lulu Enterprises, 2012), 108.

15. John Stott, *Your Mind Matters* (Downers Grove, IL: InterVarsity, 2006), 52.

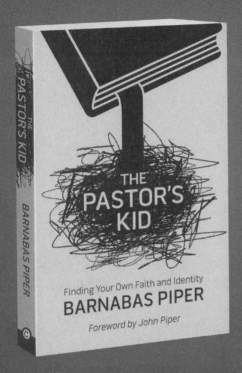

The Only One Facing as Much Pressure as the Pastor Is ...
THE PASTOR'S KID

Barnabas Piper—son of pastor and bestselling author John Piper—has experienced the challenges of being a PK firsthand. With empathy, humor, and personal stories, Piper addresses the pervasive assumptions, identity issues, and accelerated scrutiny PKs face ... and offers a path to wholeness and freedom.

David C Cook

transforming lives together